Borders Railway
The Return Journey

Peter Ross

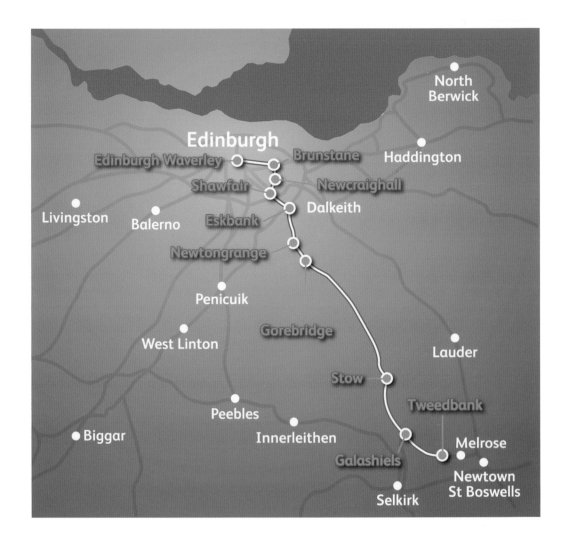

lilypublications.co.uk

ISBN 978-1-907945-90-8

The rights of Peter Ross to be identified as the author of this work have been asserted in accordance with the Copyright Act 1991.

Produced in the Isle of Man
by Lily Publications Ltd.

Edinburgh • Midlothian • Scottish Borders

This book was written by Peter Ross on behalf of the Borders Railway Project. The views Peter expresses are his own and are not intended to represent the views of the Borders Railway Project partners.

We could not even hope to feature every team or every project in the pages of this book but what we hope we've captured through Peter Ross's observations and through Peter Devlin and Robert Perry's images is the enormous sense of achievement felt within the project team and within the community as a whole.

Produced by Craig Bowman, Network Rail.

Published by Lily Publications.

Special thanks to Stuart Mackay, Sarah Duignan and all the members of the team that contributed to making this book a reality.

The Borders Railway partners are:

Network Rail, BAM, ScotRail, The Scottish Government (Transport Scotland), Midlothian Council, Scottish Borders Council and City of Edinburgh Council.

CONTENTS

KEITH BROWN
CABINET SECRETARY FOR INFRASTRUCTURE, INVESTMENT AND CITIES

The construction of the Borders Railway has been one of the biggest infrastructure undertakings Scotland has seen in living memory.

Not for over a century has a single domestic railway of its length been built in the whole of the UK, and it represents the most effectual and stunning reversal of the cuts inflicted on our railways by the infamous Dr Beeching back in the 1960s.

I have been fortunate to have been there for each of the major milestones as the route has been physically resurrected, but I recognise that it has been a far longer and more arduous journey for some than that I have travelled since construction started in April 2013.

The campaign started even before the original Waverley Line was shut down in 1969.

When Beeching's closure plans were announced, a campaign quickly took flight with a petition of over 11,000 signatures being presented at 10 Downing Street and making a heroine of local woman Madge Elliot.

Although they were sadly unsuccessful in the battle to save the line, the campaigners were tenacious and continued their fight for more than 30 years until this Scottish Government signed off plans to rebuild the line.

We took that decision because we know the value of the railways. We are overseeing a period that has been widely reported as a renaissance of the golden age of rail in Scotland, with annual passenger growth and unparalleled investment.

The Borders Railway was, for us, a project that was clearly of huge value.

I've been honoured to have been the Government Minister who was finally able to bring that dream to fruition, but also to get to know people like Madge Elliot and the other campaigners, as well as the men and women who have worked so hard over the past two and a half years to ensure this railway was brought to life.

And, as a native of Edinburgh, I've been able to develop a real and lasting connection with Midlothian and the Borders throughout this project.

These communities are now looking forward to a future with more vibrant and exciting opportunities for work, for education and study, and to make the most of those new tourism and social connections.

The opening of the Borders Railway opens up countless opportunities for the local economies and will deliver a tourism and investment boost for the whole of Scotland.

Thanks to the railway, more businesses now have the impetus to set up in Midlothian, more tourists have easier access to the Borders and the pressure is being eased on Edinburgh's housing market. Enterprises operating in all three

local authority areas before the opening are now exposed to a bigger marketplace than ever before.

It's not only an exciting time for the Borders, Midlothian and Edinburgh, it's one of the most lively and vibrant period in the history of the railways in Scotland, and Borders Railway is the jewel in that crown.

It is the legacy not only of campaigners like Madge Elliot, but of the many thousands who have been involved in the work to resurrect this great railway – from the politicians and local authority workers who saw it through the many stages of legislation to the engineers and labourers who sweated over the platforms and tracks.

And they can all take great pride as they watch the Borders Railway fuel a revival of the local communities to become thriving hubs of enterprise and tourism that will be the final nail in the coffin of the Beeching philosophy.

Although the Borders Railway seemed to spend a long time in incubation, the last two years have seen an intensive period of construction which has seen the new route sprout across the landscape of Midlothian and the central Scottish Borders.

While almost every week marked a new milestone for the project, my abiding memory will be of the people of Gala who lined the route as our rail installation machine completed its slow, relentless journey towards Tweedbank. Men and women, boys and girls, grandparents and grandchildren took up every conceivable vantage point, peering through the fencing as the final few miles of track were clipped into place.

It was a moment that helped reinforce my view that this railway will be a success.

On 6 November 2012, the day that Network Rail picked up the reins of the Borders Railway, I attended a community drop-in meeting at the National Mining Museum in Newtongrange. Despite the widespread news coverage that construction was about to start, I heard three different people that day repeating the words that had become a decade long mantra for Borders Railway – "I'll believe it when I see it".

Two and a half years on, I hope that seeing is believing.

From the outset, Network Rail, BAM and our sub-contractors have been focussed on restoring this well-loved railway line on time and within budget. We have not been without our challenges, but I'm pleased to be able to deliver the railway, as planned, in September 2015.

The achievements of the team are too many to list here, but, I hope that, in the pages of this book, we have captured the essence of what has made this job special. The project employed over 1,100 men and women at its peak and I'm proud of their achievements and hope that they are proud to have been part of this project.

I must also acknowledge the

patience and generosity of communities and individual property owners right along the route. Building a major civil engineering project is not an exact science and rarely without disruption and so has it proved with Borders Railway.

Borders Railway has added a new collection of towns, villages and hamlets to a long list of railway neighbours. Those communities will undoubtedly be relieved that construction has reached a close and I hope that the familiar rhythm of passing trains once again becomes part of the landscape of the area. For drivers using the A7, our construction traffic and traffic management has now been removed, to be replaced by a much safer, cleaner, faster transport option alongside this busy road.

Throughout the project, the team has been overwhelmed by the interest in the railway. We have been very grateful for the kind words of encouragement and delighted by the excitement and anticipation which the railway has created.

I would like to thank those who came to say hello and ask questions at our community events and elsewhere, and to all those who followed us online from around the world and took the time to learn about the project.

Despite our best efforts to fill hard disks and boxes with mountains of paperwork, there was no way that we could neatly capture every detail of this complex project. Instead, we invited Peter Ross, an award winning journalist and author, onto site to understand the work we do and the communities along the route for himself. His words, accompanied by photographs captured by Peter Devlin and Robert Perry, capture a historic moment in time and hopefully offer a bit of insight into what it was like to build the Borders Railway.

For me, the Borders Railway marks my final project before retirement. When I began my career in the railways in the 1970s, old railway infrastructure was still being removed. I'm pleased that, more than four decades on, that trend is finally being reversed. Please enjoy your new railway, it was a privilege to be asked to build it and the best possible way to finish my career.

Hugh Wark
Project Director, Network Rail

Photography:
Robert Perry and
Peter Devlin.

THEY call it the Navvies' Graveyard. A forlorn and little known spot between the South Lanarkshire villages of Elvanfoot and Crawford, at the side of fledgling Clyde, it goes unnoticed by most who roar past on the M74. Yet turn off the motorway, park up on a back road, pick your way down a steep bank and you are there – one of the secret sites of Scotland's industrial history. It looks like a fairy ring, a circle of cairns linked by rusty chains, and within it a rickle of stones from the river bed, worn and mossy and sinking into the sodden earth. These mark the graves of the 37 Irish workers who died here, in 1847, of typhus, while building the Caledonian Railway, connecting London to Glasgow and Edinburgh, through many hard miles of bleak countryside. We do not know their names.

Today, in our modern era of comprehensive employment records kept digitally, the identities of the men and women who build our railways cannot simply vanish. But in another sense they are as invisible and lost to history as those navvies of yesteryear. Given how vital construction work is to both the infrastructure and economy of the UK, it is incredible how little heed we pay to it. Yes, we grumble when projects run over budget, and we girn when we are held up by road works on our daily commute, but the actual business of building things, and the lives of those who make it their business to do so; the workers out there in the cold and the muck – well, to those we give little thought. Every capital project is an

Excavation of Edinburgh city bypass begins during an early phase of the project.

CONSTRUCTION

unmarked grave in that sense. Each gleaming tower or railway bridge or mile of road is a memorial to those who toiled upon it, but whose names are never those engraved on the brass plaque unveiled by visiting dignitaries.

That is why spending time embedded with the workers of the Borders Railway, as they grafted some miles north-east of their brethren buried in the Navvies' Graveyard – is a privilege but also a responsibility.

These are the people who for the last three years have been constructing the 31 miles of railway connecting Edinburgh to Tweedbank. To try to get them down on paper, while they themselves work in concrete and steel, may seem like an insubstantial, even petty task. One could argue, however, that it is important in its way. They have built the rails that will carry us from the rolling hills to the thronging city, and vice-versa, for generations to come. It is to be hoped that these words will carry them at least a little way into the future. Nothing lasts forever. If the lesson of the Waverley Route teaches us anything, it is that. The wonderful old term for a railway track, "the permanent way", has, too often, been made ironic as sleepers and rails were ripped up and lines closed down.

This book, then, is an attempt to record for history a historic venture. As more than one worker will tell you, with undisguised pride, "This is the biggest new railway built in Britain for over 100 years."

How do you build a railway? In 21st century Scotland it requires computer modelling and environmental consultation and safety briefings and community relations and no end of high-tech plant. But it also takes the same things it has done since the 19th century – brains and muscle and sweat and a seeming endless willingness, even a masochistic desire, to stand out in the rain and wind for days and years in order to make the damn thing happen. It takes grit.

You could, if you wished, tell the story of the Borders Railway in numbers. Construction costs: £294 million. Stations built: seven. Total number of sleepers laid: 95,834. Total tonnage of earth moved: 1,500,000. Some 10 kilometres of new road. Forty-two new bridges constructed, 95 bridges refurbished, the Gala Water crossed eighteen times; various other rivers and burns a further ten. All of this done by 1,000 workers or thereabouts, fuelled by an approximate 40,000 bacon rolls, and fags innumerable. Statistics, though, only tell part of the story. What it comes down to is this: folk.

Let's start with two of them – Hugh Wark and Martin 'Paddy' Power.

Both men work for Network Rail, the company delivering the project; BAM Nuttall is the main contractor. Paddy, the assistant construction manager, reckons he's one of the longest served railway workers on the east coast in Scotland.

Opposite:
Hugh Wark, Project Director, Network Rail.

Forty years he's been at the job, starting off in 1975 as an apprentice joiner with British Rail, God rest its soul, but his connection – as the son of a railwayman – goes back further still. As a young child he was taken on the Waverley Route, and on visits to Leith Central, where his father Frank seemed to know everybody, and so he grew up with steam and oil in his blood, and it seemed natural, when the time came, that he would work on the tracks.

Ironically, his earliest task was to remove infrastructure – station buildings, signal boxes etc – along the Waverley Route, that famous line from Edinburgh to Carlisle having closed just six years before. "For five year, six year, we just went about knocking things down," he says. "We went vandalising." This memory comes with a side-order of guilt, meaning Paddy's involvement in the construction of the Borders Railway is, in part, a form of personal reparation; restorative justice.

"The Waverley Line should never have closed," he says. "We're righting a wrong

Paddy Power,
Network Rail.

that shouldn't have happened in the first place. These communities have suffered: Galashiels; Hawick. And all the branch lines off of the Waverley Line: Kelso; Selkirk. They are isolated.

"There's a sense of achievement in putting that right. You're opening a line that will benefit folk, hopefully, for the next hundred years or more. Communities and jobs. It's going to open up the Borders. You're leaving a legacy. Like the men who first built the railway."

One morning, in the spring of 2012, Paddy Power set out to walk the route of what would become the Borders Railway. He did not go alone. He was in the company of the big boss, Hugh Wark, and they walked the 30 miles over four days. "There's no many in Hugh's position would do that," says Paddy. "But it's important to see what you're up against."

Wark is a slender, serious man of 60. Some find him intimidating; he's good, it's said, at expressing himself with a single glare. But he also inspires a great deal of loyalty, in part because no one knows the project more intimately, and because he's seen to put in a hard shift – commuting to the Newtongrange office from Perth each day, he is always among the first to arrive and the last to leave.

Being the head of a project like this must be extremely stressful at times, verging on overwhelming. All that money, all those workers, all the earth to be moved and tracks to be laid and structures to be built, and the endless, endless potential for things to go wrong. It requires the person in charge to have certain personal characteristics including steeliness (that famously articulate glare) as well as a certain serenity of thought and an ability to think in the abstract. It is also important, though, to be conversant with the physical reality of the railway. So Wark walked the line in order to understand the challenges of the route, to tread ground into memory, so that its features, each crumbling bridge and patch of bog, became something real which could be called to mind; not simply a code on a surveyor's chart. But it was not what you would call a pleasant stroll.

"It was very difficult," he recalls. "The vast majority of the line had been allowed to grow wild, or it had been taken over by adjacent farmers and estate owners. There was a lot of fencing up, and many bridges had been demolished, so there wasn't a clear path. There was bits of the route that were flooded, and we even came across some wild cattle that wouldn't let us pass. I have to pinch myself when I see it now with tracks down and construction locomotives and wagons trundling along the line."

Wark grew up in Ayrshire, a railway enthusiast from a young age, and has worked in the industry since leaving school. He's a civil engineer. Previous credits include being in charge of the construction of the Airdrie-Bathgate line and the modernisation of the Scottish leg of the west coast main line. He was attracted to this project not just because of its tempting complexity – how the hell to push through all that difficult countryside, those steep gradients, and the barrier of the Edinburgh city by-pass? – but also because the route itself is, in trainspotterish circles, such an icon. To build a line on the very land where the Waverley Route once ran is the railway engineering equivalent of covering a classic pop record. How apt, then, that for Wark the Borders Railway will also be the closing number of his working life.

"I'm retiring after this," he reveals. "This is my swan song. It's great to finish my career by reopening this fantastic bit of railway."

* * *

NOVEMBER 23rd, 2013. That, supposedly, is the date, and we are, supposedly, in Scotland. But it could be France, 1916. The muddy ground is rutted and churned, chewed up by the big earth-movers, and frozen hard with ice. Frost glints on tangles of wire and a few blasted-looking silver birches. Someone makes the usual joke about the Battle of the Somme. It's a standard line round here. Just twelve days ago, worked stopped for the two minute silence to mark Armistice Day, and the Borders Railway workers, in mute observance, felt a grim solidarity with the poor bloody infantrymen of almost a century before. Okay, no one here is getting shot or shelled, but the dirt and the cold are the same. Carve these words on the stone flanks of the Hardengreen flyover: *Dulce et decorum est pro patria molior*.

This morning it is minus six. In temperatures like that you are glad to work. We are standing in what will become, eventually, the Shawfair cutting. The earthworks, they say, are already eighty-six per cent completed. But it's still hard to see this as a railway. One of the senior men points back north in the direction of a bright red buffer. "The first new bit of track will be laid down there." The buffer marks the point where the new railway will connect with the existing line out of Edinburgh.

The first six months of work was spent "de-vegging" the route: removing all the trees and bushes and other vegetation that had grown up through the old track in the decades since closure. Thirty miles of that to a width of fifteen metres. Trees, of course, weren't the only things in the way. Homes, too. Some 35 residential properties were demolished along the route, the vast majority acquired through compulsory purchase orders.

For its first two kilometres or so out of Edinburgh, the Borders Railway is entirely new, following a route to the west of the old Waverley Line, in order to provide transport links for a huge new development of 4,000 new homes as well as schools and shops at Shawfair. The upshot of this is that the track passes over the Midlothian coalfield, where the earth is pitted like a peach stone. Mining here goes back centuries, back to the monks of Newbattle. Men have long hewn the ground for its riches, and now, with the coming of the railway, the task was to fill in the pits on which so many had laboured for so long.

Ground investigation work discovered thirteen old mineshafts in the Monktonhall

Muddy conditions at Hardengreen.

area alone. If these were laid end to end on the surface, they would stretch from Edinburgh to Manchester. Finding them and dealing with them is crucial in order to avoid future subsidence, but it isn't easy. Nineteenth century maps were consulted, local knowledge tapped; older folk were literally asked, "Where were the mines round here?" Shallow excavations uncovered a few black and gaping mouths. Once a shaft was discovered, the area was sealed off in case of collapse, and the work of filling it began. Grout, a mix of cement and pulverised fuel ash, was pumped in by giant orange drilling rigs. There's something hellish about the sight. In the vicinity of the old Gore pit, near Gorebridge, steam rose from the hot grout as it was forced deep into the unwilling earth.

Perhaps the most complex, high-stakes and nerve-shredding of all the works on the Borders project has been the building of a railway bridge beneath the Edinburgh City Bypass near the Sheriffhall roundabout. This meant the construction of a temporary dual-carriageway while the structure was built, and then the eventual switch back to the original alignment. All the work had to be done smoothly and to tight deadlines so that the road remained fully open at peak times. Any mistake or delay would have meant effectively closing off the mass of traffic coming to and from the Borders and the A1 to England.

"Can you imagine this not opening up on the Monday morning?" says Paddy Power, sweeping a hand towards the roaring commuter traffic. "Can you imagine the chaos and the havoc and the bad publicity? That's the nightmare scenario. You can get an idea of the pressure on everybody. It always comes down the line: 'Whose fault is this?' So everybody was mucking in to get the road open."

An additional sense of jeopardy came from the knowledge that the data cable for a major bank, carrying critical information about UK and international transactions, runs underground right where the tunnelling beneath the bypass was due to be carried out. "If we broke it," one worker recalls, "we could have affected the cost of the pound." This, for most of us, would be the stuff of cold sweats and waking screaming in the night. But railway workers with the right stuff see it differently.

"It was," says a young engineer, "a total adrenalin rush."

The Borders Railway project was divided into three areas of construction – North, Central and South – with work proceeding simultaneously in each. The North extends from Shawfair to the former pit village Gorebridge. The Central section carries on to just before the giant Bowshank Tunnel, a place of Stygian darkness a few miles of south of Stow. The final section is everything from the tunnel to the terminus at Tweedbank, south-east of Galashiels. The cliched view which regards the Scottish Borders as being isolated, insular, lawless and rather Here Be Dragons extends, among railway workers, to those of their colleagues based in the south. Enquiries about the section are met with a wry shake of the head: "You've mair chance o' findin' oot whit's gaun oan in North Korea." Had Scotland voted for independence, the joke went, the south section crew were contracted to build a wall across the border.

A word about the Bowshank Tunnel. One of two historic tunnels on the line, the other being Torwoodlee, a little further south, Bowshank is 200 metres of lovely atmospheric gloom deep within a hillside; one hesitates to give metric measurements for such a venerable Victorian lady, so let us add that she is approximately seven yards wide by seven high.

A cast-iron lattice bridge carries the track over the Gala and into the tunnel from the north. Declarations of young love, and eternal allegiance to Heart of Midlothian FC, have been scratched into the sides of this bridge, but there is

Opposite:
Crowds gather at Galashiels for rail installation.

barely time to read them before the gaze is drawn, gravitationally, to the black hole of the entrance and the grand brick vault beyond. "Talk about a micro-climate," one tunneller laughed grimly. "I've walked in there in bright sunshine, come out the other side and it's pishin' doon."

Inside, in the chill spring of 2014, as orange-suited workers dug down into the bedrock to create room for a new concrete floor, cold wet clay sucked at boots and spirits; not quite a year later, the tunnel flashed and sparked as steel tracks were laid and cut, the shadows of the workers dancing on the walls. What a job it must have been to dig this place out. Miserable and dangerous. In April 1847, a navvy was killed in a fall of earth. Historic accounts of tunnelling elsewhere on the Waverley Route describe water pouring through the ceiling and the struggle to pump enough air to the men. Bowshank has always been a cold place; infamous for its icicles. "You had to keep your head in the cab or you could lose an eye," one former steam engine driver recalled. "If a train hadn't been through for a while, you would be breaking the icicles as you went."

Bowshank, though hardly cosy for railway workers, is a tremendously well-appointed abode if you happen to be a bat. Ecologists connected to the project installed "bat flaps" to encourage the animals to leave the tunnel ahead of work commencing, and provided alternative roost sites in nearby trees. Three licensed "bat workers" on the project carried out around 2,000 surveys on the structures of the railway – the bridges, tunnels and so on – while other ecologists paid particular attention to the welfare of badgers, otters and nesting birds. There were 173 badger setts discovered along the route of the railway; artificial replacements were built and the creatures rehomed.

Even the less beloved and attractive forms of animal life have been taken into account. When, in late 2013, a 250 metre stretch of the Gala Water at Heriot was diverted temporarily in order to minimise the risk of pollution, seventy or so lamprey – a nightmarishly hideous jawless fish – were caught using a method called "electrofishing". Stunned by electricity, but unharmed, they floated to the surface where they were netted and moved to another part of the river. The Victorian railway builders would, no doubt, be astonished that such things were considered, but this is what goes into 21st century construction. Life is no longer cheap. Not even the life of a lamprey.

* * *

NOVEMBER 13th, 2014. Dawn is breaking and Rab Kenny, a section foreman in the north section, is about to set off down the A7 in his Ford pick-up. But first he has calls to make – reassuring himself that his men know what they are supposed to get done that day. A posh automated voice announces who's being dialled, the Scots names sounding odd and exotic in the Bluetooth's blue-blood accent: "Calling to Jock"; "Calling to Shug"; "Calling to Malky". Blunt-faced, sleepy-eyed, a fleshy pile of muscle and stubble, Rab has his name tattooed on his left hand, and "bam" written across the back of his jacket. At first you might think that word describes his nature rather than his employer – BAM Nuttall – but not at all. This man is solid, dependable, impressive; a leader. He started out "on the shovel", as he puts it, and at 47 has worked his way up. A construction project is not unlike a military campaign; each has a chain of command. Rab is thus akin to an army colour sergeant – still very much in touch with the boots on the ground but with an eye on the larger strategy and intelligent marshalling of resources. "It's like running a war," he says.

He's in charge of around 30 men, including five "gangers", the foremen for each party of labourers. He wears his seniority lightly, but no one ever doubts it. That he addresses everyone as "son" only adds to his patrician air. "You've got to be a bit of a peace-maker, a bit of a father-figure. You've got to be able to read the boys' minds – who's on an upper, who's on a downer. Sometimes you've got to whip, but that's not my style."

This is his way of talking. Philosophical, but rough and ready. He has developed a sort of Gaffer's Tao: "Even when there's nothin' tae dae, there's always somethin' tae dae"; "Never kick a man's arse in the mornin' in case it's the arse you have to kiss at night". Rab lives in a caravan in Galashiels and cooks a lot of stovies.

It's worth describing a day with Rab and his crew because he seems representative, in his manner and methods, of the workers and the work on the Borders Railway. One stands for all. The way he gets things done appears to be, largely, the way things got done everywhere.

The main task for the day is the construction of a concrete footbridge over the tracks, the replacement for a path which until recently connected Gorebridge with an area of woodland. The columns are already in place and it is now a question of placing the landing units on top of these, easing them down over the steel spikes which will lock them into place. Each of these five landings is a sort of inverted concrete pyramid, the approximate size of a 4x4 truck. Moving them requires a huge crane, but first the crane has to be manoeuvred into position, and that's a job in itself.

Construction work is often described as a giant jigsaw puzzle. The trick is to

make sure there's no pieces left over at the end of the day. An outsider could be forgiven for detecting a certain casual fatalism among the workers when it comes to schedules. "Yon time," for instance, is the standard unit of temporal measurement, as in, "What time will we be here till the night?" "Och, yon time." It is the workie equivalent of mañana. Yet without careful planning and a great deal of stress and sweat, no deadline would ever be met. The trick seems to be to cleave ruthlessly to a timetable while giving the impression to the world that there's plenty of time to lean on your spade and enjoy a fly smoke. It is a matter of keeping down appearances.

Getting the crane into place by the bridge is Rab's first headache. It has to be driven down a steep dirt track and round a tight bend, and the operator from the sub-contractor – a man mountain called Russell – doesn't fancy it at all. He's worried about damaging the vehicle, about getting stuck at the bottom of the hill, and he adopts a firm position from the outset. "This is a f***in' disgrace," he says. "There's no f***in' way I'm goin' doon there. It's as simple as f***in' that."

Rab, though, is a diplomat. "C'mon," he says, talking through mouthfuls of roll and sausage. "Let's no' throw the toys oot the pram."

This goes on for a while until a compromise is reached. Russell will drive the crane down the track which will then be landscaped so that its slope is gentler and he can get back up when the work is over. None of these negotiations are carried out in raised voices; the language is aggressive but not the tone. This sort of stand-off, clearly, is a daily occurrence. Just part of the job. Fascinating, though – like watching two stags sizing each other up. "Aye," nods Rab. "It's aboot seein' who's got the biggest set of baws."

The crane really is enormous, by the way – 220 tonnes, each wheel the height of a small man – and to see it at work is a delight. What's striking is how graceful it is for such a beast. Russell, clearly, is an artist; the Diaghilev of the jib. He performs a lovely pas de deux with a cherry-picker, the arms of the two vehicles swinging past each other in slow delicate arcs as they lift and place the concrete platforms on the columns. They get the first one up in just 22 minutes and you feel like applauding, if only to release the tension. The six men manoeuvring the platforms into place have seven tonnes above their heads and it is a nervous moment as it descends into place. "The eagle has landit," says someone as it comes to rest, and there's relief in the answering laughter.

Space exploration is in the air. It is the day after the European Space Agency's Rosetta mission landed a probe on a moving comet, and there has been much hilarity among the railway workers that it bounced out of radio contact. The

Opposite:
Rab Kenny, BAM.

suggestion that placing these concrete platforms on the columns of the footbridge is, in some ways, rather like what ESA were trying to do is regarded by Rab as a happy analogy.

"Aye," he says, "but at least oors has stuck."

* * *

KEVIN Kelly puts the phone down. "Damn and shit it!" he groans. "Holy Jaysus! What other disaster will befall us before this morning's out?"

Kelly, 59, is works manager in the south. The senior man here. It is eleven days until Christmas, 2014, and the festive spirit is yet to reach the office in Galashiels where he is based. The problem is manpower. He hasn't got enough men to make the job advance at the speed he'd like. A new safety rule has come in lately, meaning that each work party must be accompanied by a non-working supervisor, known as a "yellow hat", and finding the right men to do that job, this close to the holiday, is a challenge.

Bridge beam craned into place at Wheatlands Road.

Safety has always been emphasised on the Borders Railway job, but especially so now. Towards the end of November, 49 year old worker Huw Jenkins lost one of his legs when a concrete sleeper fell on him while it was being unloaded by a crane. Work on the line stopped immediately for a review of safety systems, and by Christmas progress was four weeks behind schedule and the mood dark. The effect of the accident on the team was "stunning" according to Hugh Wark. Employees were offered advice on coping with trauma.

The incident happened on the outskirts of Galashiels and came not quite six months after a fatal road accident, also in the southern section. A tractor and trailer being driven by a 54 year old BAM Nuttall employee on the A7 was hit by a lorry and the man was killed. "A few of the lads took that hard," says Dave Siney, general foreman for the section. "I know I was affected. It is like losing one of our own."

Building a railway is a difficult, delicate equation with several variables. Manpower, morale, money, time, the landscape, the climate. All of that goes into it and there is, all the time, enormous pressure. A railway has a kind of brute inevitability. There is something dumb and insistent about it. It *will* be built. The men who build it give various reasons for their doing so. They do it for the pay, of course, but sometimes also out of a sense of pride, or because they find the work interesting and fulfilling, or because they are the fourth generation to work on the railway and they have tracks in their blood. Deeper than that, though, what you detect is a sense of destiny, a sense that they are thirled to the work. They are building the railway because they are building a railway, and what else would they do?

So, despite the accidents and the upset they caused, despite whatever God and the devil in charge of the Scottish weather choose to throw at the project, no one has any doubt that the work will be completed on time and that trains, before long, will arrive in Galashiels for the first time in almost half a century.

"It will get done," says Kevin Kelly. "We'll do it because we always do."

* * *

FEBRUARY 2nd, 2015. Sander den Ouden, a big 36 year old from Utrecht, leads the way along the track, walking towards the sun rising over the Eildon hills, stepping on the sleepers, pausing sometimes to stoop and chalk marks on the rails where they are to be welded. There is snow on the ballast, and his men, when we meet them, are wearing balaclavas beneath their helmets, e-fags poking out and giving them the look of grizzled Daleks.

For the last four months these dozen men have walked the route of the railway, laying the track with a special machine shipped over from Holland. It was T-shirt weather when they started out, but as the weeks have passed they have gradually added layers until each is a sort of thermal Michelin Man. They have walked through the best and worst of the Scottish weather. They have had to clear snow from the sleepers before the track could be laid. And now, at last, they are just four days away from the end of the job. Today is a milestone: they will reach Galashiels. The track-laying machine, in honour of the nationalities of the men who work on it, is decorated with Saltires and the flag of the Netherlands. Someone has painted a motto along the front: "For the finishing touch God created the Dutch!"

Lengths of track, each 108 metres and weighing six tonnes, are offloaded from a wagon which follows the machine and then fed through its winches, wheels and levers until laid upon the sleepers, at which point the men clip them into place. In this way, they can, in theory, lay the best part of a mile each day, but of course there are hold-ups and slow-downs. The previous Friday, the ballast train derailed at Bowland, setting everything back.

In such circumstances, it is important to keep the mood up, and so the men maintain a good supply of pork pies, Irn-Bru and craic. The Dutch workers have, of an evening, been introduced to those delights of Scottish cuisine – haggis

suppers and Tennent's lager – and have tried valiantly to understand a single word that is being said to them.

All of the men, Scottish and Dutch, have been moved by the emotional response of the public they have encountered along the way. "Last week, I seen a woman crying," says Paul Morris, a huge worker, from the depths of his black hood. "She was standing on that bridge back there. It means that much to people, so you take a pride in it, aye." He takes his phone out of his pocket to show black and white photos of steam trains passing under the very bridge where he is working now. "This is historic," he says. He can feel the history with every rail he puts down.

Especially in the Borders, where the closure of the Waverley Route is often regarded as a historic injustice, feelings run high and crowds line up beside the fences to watch the track laid down. Some of these people are hungry for souvenirs and some of the workers are happy to supply them. John King, known as Johnny One Cut is a 40 year old from Musselburgh and the man on this crew who works the rail saw. His job is to cut the lengths of laid rails so they end in the middle of the sleeper. As he bends and grinds, sparks shower up, and he is left each time with a small length of steel which, in profile, looks a little like a chess pawn. These are coveted items amongst trainspotters and other enthusiasts for the line, and King is only half joking when he takes a red marker pen and signs one – J1C – before dropping it at his feet. The artist has autographed his latest creation, and it isn't long before this particular piece of sculpture finds a home.

It makes its way into the hands of David Romanis. "Oh!" he says, fair delighted. "That'll get pride of place."

Romanis, 65, and his wife, Violet, have made the short trip east from Clovenfords to watch the railway arrive in Galashiels. His father, Herbert, had worked as a guard on the railway for 47 years before being made redundant when the Waverley Route closed. As a young man, David wrote to the Queen and to the then Prime Minister Harold Wilson, asking for the line to be saved. But, of course, to no avail. So, why come and see this today? "Oh, it's history in the making. The line closed in January '69 and now it's coming back. It means a lot to me. My dad is long dead, but he would have been really pleased to see this day."

At precisely half past noon on February 2, 2015, the tracks pass under the Brewery Brig and are guided into place by the workers to the sound of applause from the people looking down from above. The railway has arrived in Galashiels for the first time in 46 years. This sight is witnessed by a few dozen souls braving the cold: dog-walkers, kids from the local nursery, a few curious drinkers lured from the pub; but mostly by those in their autumn years who remember the railway and are glad to see it back. For these people, this is a moment when black and white turns to colour; when their youth and old age are coupled together. They must almost be able to smell the steam. Naturally, then, no one would ruin the occasion with an uncharitable thought for rival towns that do not – yet – have their station back. Would they?

"Aye," sighs a gentle looking man of middle years, walking a Labradoodle, "the guid thing aboot this is Hawick's still screwed."

* * *

SO, it is built. Some said it never would be; others that it never should have been. There is rumoured to be an especially cynical and stubborn postman in one of the towns along the track who believes, even now, that the line will not open. Yet the Borders Railway is here, it is real, and, come September, the first trains will run on its gleaming new tracks.

They will leave Edinburgh Waverley, pass beneath the city bypass, over the magnificent Lothianbridge Viaduct with its 23 Victorian arches, plumb the Bowshank and Torwoodlee Tunnels; over the coalfield, over 42 new bridges, over the Gala and Tweed. They will pass through high land and – no doubt – hard rain, through some of Scotland's most beautiful countryside, and they will arrive at Tweedbank less than an hour after setting off.

Almost half a century has drifted by since trains were seen in these valleys and hills. A generation or two. In the lifetime of this landscape, though, it is nothing, not even a passing season. The leaves fall, the wind blows, the smoke clears, and there is a railway once more.

What the workers cannot do is build memories into those tracks. That ballast comes later. People will use these trains to go to work, to meet lovers, to end affairs. They will travel to weddings, to funerals, to ceilidhs and wakes. They will hold the hands of children and elderly parents, and perhaps they will talk about the steam trains that used to run here, or perhaps they will not. Perhaps they will keep their head buried in their paper and think nothing of what was lost and the labour – the sheer sweat and skill – that has gone into bringing it back. But the workers will know. They will feel it in their muscles for a while yet, and they will hold it in their minds forever.

"You're leaving a legacy," said Paddy Power. "We'll do it because we always do," said Kevin Kelly. That's what it's all about. Faith and hope. Two things you need on any journey. For the Borders Railway, this latest is just about to begin ...

Jock Wallace, BAM.

Adam Craig, BAM.

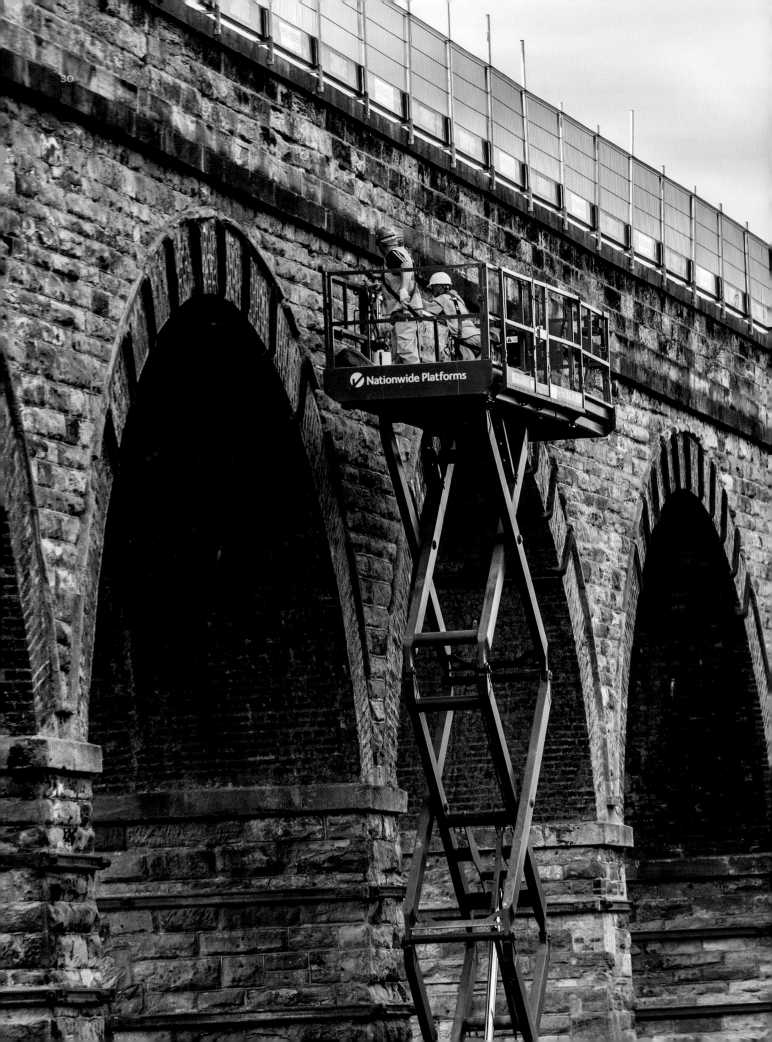

Nationwide Platforms

Restoration of a Railway
A PHOTOGRAPHIC JOURNEY

Photos: Peter Devlin
Aerial photography: White House Studios

Mining Remediation

North of Edinburgh city bypass, the Borders Railway follows a divergent route to that of the Waverley Line, which closed in 1969. To help regenerate a former industrial brownfield site, the line was plotted to run through the site of the former Monktonhall Colliery, which closed in 1997 but had been the site of ancient mine works for up to 500 years.

Before earthworks could begin, ground stabilisation was essential to reduce the possibility of future subsidence. Ground investigation works uncovered around 30 mine shafts, 10 of which directly affected the railway corridor. Over 4,000 tonnes of grout were used to fill the underground voids and minimise risk to the new railway.

Earthworks

Where possible, excavated material, such as rock was re-used in other locations. At Falahill, rock was excavated from site, reducing the need to import rock from other locations and keeping haulage miles to a minimum.

August 2013: Generally speaking, the Borders Railway project was blessed by fine weather, however, the odd wet spell was inevitable, resulting in damp conditions in August 2013, as city bypass diversion works got underway.

October 2013: The latter half of 2013 saw earth works begin in other locations along the route, including Langlee in Galashiels. Langlee was one of numerous locations along the route where the former railway solum was filled-in following the closure of the Waverley Route in 1969.

Falahill

March 2014: The scale of excavation work at Falahill brought into perspective

City Bypass

September 2013 – No through road: as work begins to excavate the city bypass, barriers are removed from the road-side.

OVERLEAF: City bypass (A720): One of the single largest obstacles on the route was the city bypass which carries in excess of 40,000 cars per day. To avoid serious disruption to traffic, the road needed to remain open throughout construction. The solution was to construct a 400m long, four lane diversion alongside the original road. This allowed engineers to cut down through the city bypass, construct the new bridge structure, fill and rebuild the road.

   Once complete, the diverted section of road was removed and the railway infrastructure was built underneath the bypass.

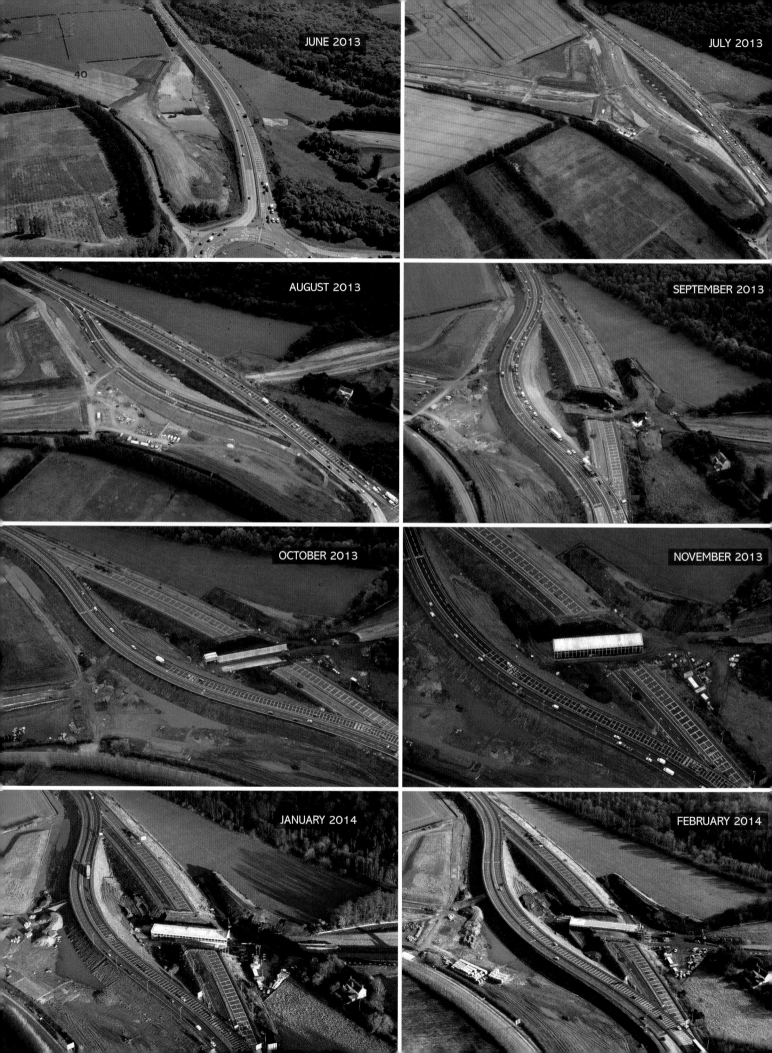

JUNE 2013

JULY 2013

AUGUST 2013

SEPTEMBER 2013

OCTOBER 2013

NOVEMBER 2013

JANUARY 2014

FEBRUARY 2014

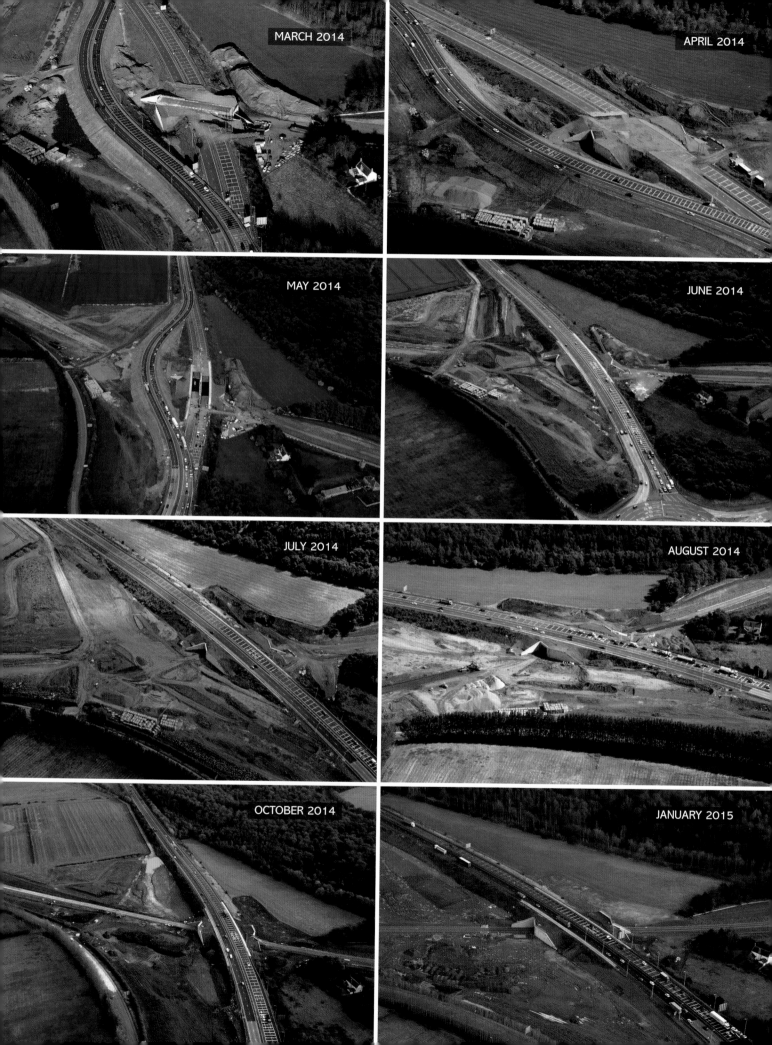

October 2013 - Structure begins to emerge from the cutting created through the busy arterial route.

May 2014 - Substantially complete, the new bridge awaits road surfacing and finishing works.

Lothianbridge Viaduct

Lothianbridge Viaduct is the largest masonry structure on the route and, at 23 arches long, easily the largest old structure to be put back into use. Despite the foliage growing from the bridge deck and from gaps in the masonry, this grand old bridge was found to be in good condition. Railings along the bridge parapets were beyond repair and needed to be replaced, while some masonry and pointing work needed attention. The bridge deck, however, was sound, requiring very little in the way of refurbishment.

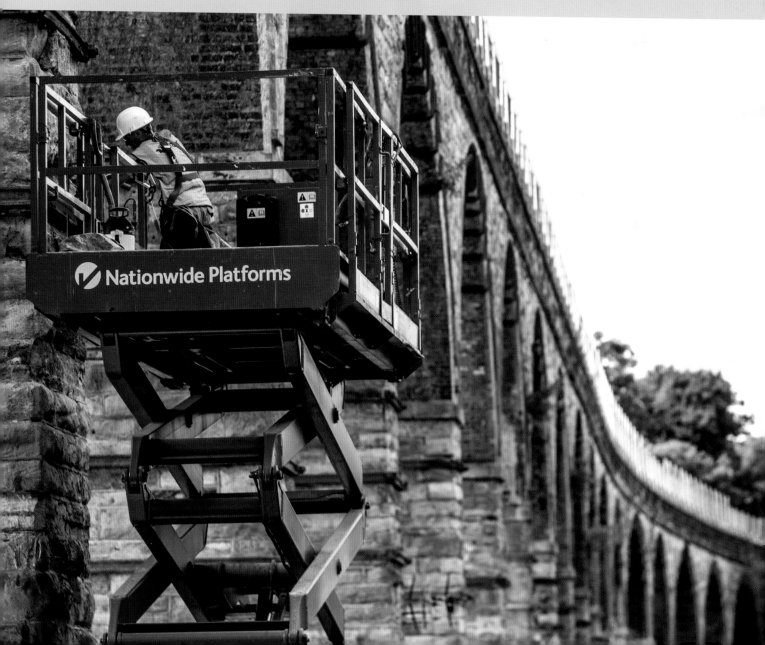

1st
access
Rentals
01698 732418

Bridges

Bridges are a characteristic feature of the new Borders Railway route, largely thanks to the line's close proximity to a variety of rivers including the North Esk, Gala Water and the Tweed.

While 42 entirely new structures required construction, using a variety of modern techniques, the character of the old Waverley Route remains intact thanks to considerate design and innovative preservation.

Ultimately, 95 structures were retained in full or in part.

HARDENGREEN

At 71.5 metres long, Hardengreen Viaduct is the longest new structure on the route. The structure was required to span the A7 at Hardengreen roundabout where the railway route was breeched in 1991 by road improvement works.

Building the structure was logistically challenging due to its proximity to the A7. Ultimately, road traffic was only disrupted for two weekends in early 2014, as four 104 tonne pre-cast concrete beams were craned into position. They were fixed to three support columns built on site.

HARELAW

Harelaw footbridge – the forty-second and final new bridge to be installed along the Borders Railway was craned into position on 7 April 2015. An additional 95 old bridges were refurbished to bring them up to standard.

HOGBACK BRIDGES

Wrought iron hog-back bridges: A distinguishing feature of the Borders Railway, great effort was taken to repair and preserve these 12 wrought iron bridges which help the railway criss-cross the Gala Water

Although bridge decks were in a poor state of repair, the metal structures were found to be structurally sound. To bring them back to an acceptable standard, the bridges were encapsulated before being grit blasted and painted. New bridge decks and hand rails were installed before the railway was laid.

WHEATLANDS ROAD

One of the most complex new structures in the
south section of the route was the Wheatlands
Road bridge. All bridges in Gala were painted 'Gala
Maroon', as stipulated by Scottish Borders Council.
The colour has historic relevance back to the days
of the Borders Reivers.

Falahill

One of three locations where the A7 and railway cross, Falahill was undoubtedly the most challenging and contentious location along the route.

The crossing design delivered by the project went through two earlier iterations before the final scheme was agreed. The revised design saw the railway pass under the road to the south of Falahill cottages, with the A7 realigned to the north to allow more room for those properties.

Land owned by the project at Falahill was also identified as offering a plentiful source of rock for the project. The site was quarried extensively throughout the duration of the project, with materials used in locations right along the route.

This approach made sound financial and environmental sense, however, it presented challenging temporary circumstances for A7 users and Falahill residents, some of whom chose to accept the project's offer of voluntary purchase.

The quarry site has since been filled and landscaped.

Tunnels

Borders Railway is served by two notable tunnels, the 62m long Torwoodlee Tunnel, north of Gala and the 200m long Bowshank Tunnel, south of Stow. The Bowshank Tunnel required the most remedial work. Masonry lined walls were reinforced with spray concrete while the tunnel floor was lowered by 400mm to allow for potential future electrification and prepare for slab track installation.

Environment

April 2013 - soil samples from excavation sites all along the route were collected and tested to allow for re-use of materials and prevent contamination

October 2013 - Waterways feature prominently along the Borders Railway route. In a number of locations, the Gala Water needed to be temporarily diverted to avoid contamination by nearby excavation and construction works. Testing was carried out regularly to check for pollutants.

August 2013 - A variety of protected species feature along the Borders Railway route, including this pipistrelle bat, which was provided with an alternative roost after being excluded from Bowshank Tunnel. Other protected species included badgers, otters and lamprey.

Drainage

Research and ground investigations by the project team identified numerous locations along the route where landslips had occurred in the past. To reduce the risk of history repeating itself, and to mitigate the effects of peat bogs, marshland and saturated ground, over 100 miles of drainage were installed along the route.

This deep drain (opposite) in Galashiels was refurbished to serve the needs of the new railway.

Ground Stabilisation and Ga

Over 44 years, the former railway solum had become overgrown and cuttings were unstable. Early work required top soil to be scraped back and cuttings to be re-graded to modern standards. In many locations, earth cuttings were reinforced using a layer of rock.

Where more robust reinforcement was required, gabion baskets filled with rock were used to reduce the risk of landslips. Gabions are less costly to build than retaining walls and were used to support cuttings and embankments all along the route.

Logistics and Materials

95,834 sleepers were used to build the Borders Railway. They were delivered by rail to Millerhill before being distributed along the route. Sleepers were subsequently positioned every 650mm (26") prior to rail installation.

Above: Thousands of tonnes of ballast were used in the construction of the railway. After being delivered to Millerhill by rail, ballast for the bottom layer of track was distributed to numerous locations along the route in preparation for spreading.
Inset: Tree cutting and vegetation removal was required all along the route. Over 40 years of growth was removed during the first pass. Subsequent devegetation was carried out as the railway took shape to reduce the potential for disruption and damage caused by leaf fall and fallen branches.
Below: Utility diversions were one of the invisible elements of the project that presented serious challenges. At Langlee in Gala utilities had to be removed from Winston Road before the embankment could be removed and a new bridge built. The diverted utilities were buried under the railway.

Road Works

Over 10km of new roads were constructed as part of the project works. The bulk of new roads were built near Shawfair Station, in Midlothian, opening up this brownfield site for park and ride opportunities and future development.

In the Scottish Borders, new access roads were built in Heriot and Fountainhall, bridging the railway rather than replacing the former level crossings which featured on the former Waverley Route.

Schools Activities

Throughout the project, interaction with schools, young people and community groups was given high priority. The project reached over 1,500 pupils along the route through its safety workshops run in partnership with Scottish Youth Theatre, while BAM's 'bridges to schools' activities run with help from the Institute of Civil Engineers gave children the opportunity to receive practical instruction on the principles of bridge building.

Above: BAM Project Director Nissar Mohammed celebrates the end of construction and the firm's 150th anniversary with Stow Primary School pupils.

The project's partnership with Scottish Football Association provided children with railway safety messages through football workshops during holidays and outwith school hours.

At Stow, the primary school lies just metres from the new station. Special attention was paid to reduce the impact of rail works on the school during construction works and children were given an exclusive opportunity to see rail installation works up close when the track laying team made their way through Stow.

Signalling and Telecoms

Signalling and telecoms installation could only be carried out once the railway was effectively complete. Signals on the new route control access on and off three sections of double track and into the island platform at Tweedbank.

Stations

Masonry work to complete the station walls at Ladhope Vale, Galashiels.

Lighting column installed at Eskbank Station

GOREBRIDGE STATION

Gorebridge station is one of only two, along with Stow, which lies on the site of the original station. The original station building has been retained and will be sold on the private market following the completion of construction.

Gorebridge Station was the site of new housing and business venture following the closure of the old route in 1969. The property had to be demolished prior to building work beginning.

The station site and railway corridor required extensive excavations prior to rebuilding the station. The station building, however, has been retained and will be sold as a development opportunity following the railway's opening.

Platform works underway – Gorebridge is one of four new stations along the route with a single platform serving both north and south bound trains.

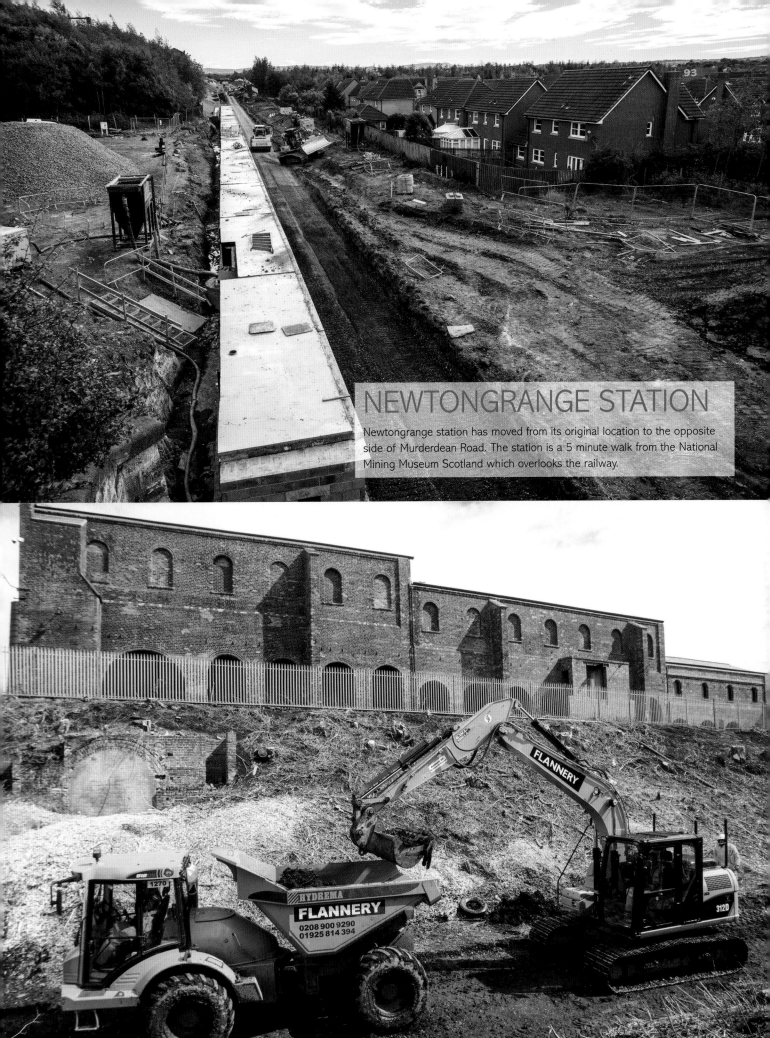

NEWTONGRANGE STATION

Newtongrange station has moved from its original location to the opposite side of Murderdean Road. The station is a 5 minute walk from the National Mining Museum Scotland which overlooks the railway.

STOW STATION

Stow is one of only two stations on Borders Railway with two platforms – Shawfair being the other. The station is sited on the west side of Stow on the site of the former station. Since the closure of the Waverley Route a Primary School has been built on an adjacent site. Minimising the impact of construction on school activities was a key priority for the project. Early in the process, a noise reduction barrier was erected to isolate the school from construction activities.

TWEEDBANK STATION

Track Laying

Track laying began on 6 October 2014 at the tie-in point near Millerhill depot. 108m length sections of rail on a purpose built wagon were pushed into position by a locomotive before being pulled out in front of the wagon by a lifting device propelled by caterpillar tracks, nicknamed the 'boojum' by some interested railway onlookers.

IF YOU HAVE A PROBLEM
IF NO ONE ELSE CAN HELP
AND IF YOU CAN FIND THEM
MAYBE YOU CAN HIRE.....
THE RAIL OFFLOADING TEAM

The rail offloading team was made up of 14 men from BAM's Dutch and Scottish teams. The team worked Monday to Friday and could lay as many as 24 108m lengths of rail every day, equalling almost 1.3km of track.

Favourable autumn weather meant that track laying made rapid progress through Midlothian. The impending arrival of the rail offloading team was a big incentive to complete the critical civil engineering works and, in some locations, sleepers were only positioned hours before the rail installation team arrived.

The rail team crossed from Midlothian into the Scottish Borders on 5 November 2015 at Cakemuir Burn. To mark the occasion, south section project manager, Ken MacGillivray (centre) welcomed Scottish Borders Council leader David Parker and chief executive Tracey Logan onto site.

Winter weather didn't put a stop to rail installation activities. Snow blowers were used to help clear the sleepers as the team crept ever closer to Gala. Ballast trains followed the rail installation team down the newly laid train, dropping a top layer of stone. Progress was delayed by a couple of days in January 2015 when cold weather froze the ballast inside the auto-hoppers.

Progress through Bowshank Tunnel made for dramatic scenes. Sections of rail needed to be cut to align them with the centre of closest sleeper. A new saw blade was required for every cut off. Each section of rail was eventually welded together to create a continuous rail, meaning a smoother journey for passengers.

The arrival of the rail installation team into Galashiels was greeted with excitement, with dozens of people lining the route to watch its progress.

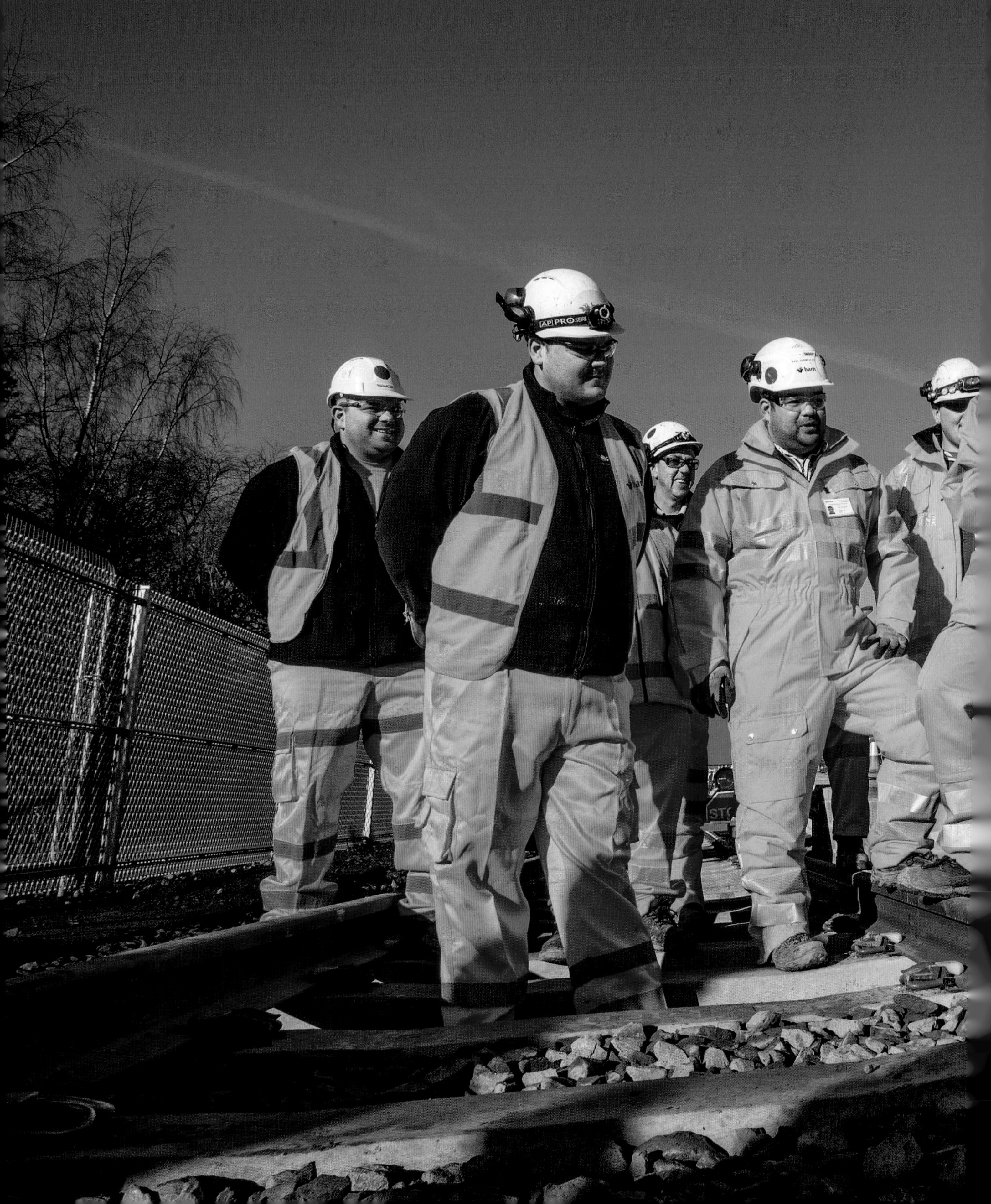

The rail installation team was joined by Keith Brown MSP, Cabinet Secretary for Infrastructure, Investment and Cities on 12 February 2015 to fit the final, golden Pandrol clip into place.

THE Borders Railway will open up areas of Scotland which, for many years, have been conveniently accessible only to those making the journey by car. It is expected that the railway will give tourism a significant boost. Midlothian has the National Mining Museum and Rosslyn Chapel; the Borders have long been famous for their beautiful ancient abbeys; and Tweedbank station will, in future, be home to the Great Tapestry of Scotland. More significant than any specific attraction, though, will be the opportunity for people from outside the area to be exposed to the wonderful culture and folk of this part of the country. This chapter celebrates both.

* * *

NEW Year's Day in Newtongrange. The town's beloved Silver Band has risen early, in cheerful defiance of Hogmanay hangovers and terrible weather, to fulfil their annual duty of marching through the streets and waking the townsfolk to a new morning, a new year.

"This village comes to life the day," says Alan Fernie, the 54 year old conductor. He is a well known and highly regarded composer and arranger who learned about music right here, taking up the trombone at the age of twelve in part to cheer up his father who had broken his leg in a mining accident. Alan now lives in Selkirk, and travels the world as a performer, but would never miss being here on January 1st. "This is a very special day. There's an atmosphere that I can't explain."

Newtongrange, known to all who live here as "Nitten", is a former mining village in Midlothian. One of the many places in this part of Scotland, as with parts of Ayrshire and Fife, which were born out of coal and must now go on living without the work which gave them money, pride and purpose. The local pit, Lady Victoria Colliery, closed in 1981 and is now the National Mining Museum. The 26 metre high headgear still dominates the skyline, but is static, a beautiful gravestone. The same could be said, for many years, of the Lothianbridge Viaduct, a landmark in the area thanks to its magnificent Victorian arches. Come September, though, the structure will once again carry trains to and fro. Newtongrange is one of seven brand new stations on the Borders Railway.

It is not quite 10am and we are in the band hall on Dalhousie Road. Old photos on the walls; banners and certificates. Handshakes and happy new years. The shush and pop of a few hairs of the dog as cans of lager are opened. Beer fragrances the musty smell of the room, as people start tuning

Photography:
Robert Perry.

up. The great earth-shaking groan of the tuba speaks for many a sore head. "Lubricates the valves," winks Duncan McCluskie, a 21 year old tuba player, taking a swig from a tin.

"This tradition has gone on for as long as I can remember, and well before that," says Angus Edmond, the principal cornet player, who has been in the band since 1979, when he was 19. "At least 100 years. There's people you'll meet today who will be able to give you an exact date; that's if they're sober enough to talk to you."

The Silver Band's official crest shows the Lady Victoria winding wheel in silhouette. Like Newtongrange itself, the band emerged from that mining culture, and although the industry is gone, they remain as ambassadors and upholders of its values – comradeship, solidarity, community, hard work and joy.

These local values are, to an extent, national values. They are Scotland's values. You can't see them. You can't look out the window of a train and admire them as they pass. But get out at Newtongrange, at Gorebridge, at Stow, at Gala – and you will sense them in many of the people you meet. This part of the country is,

for the most part, quiet and undemonstrative. The folk don't make a fuss. They just get on with it. But there is a quiet benevolence at work which matches the unshowy landscape, and do not think for a moment that these places are without passion. Visit Gorebridge on Gala Day. See in the new year in Newtongrange. Then you'll know.

"Right guys, grab your music," says Angus. "We'll need to get going."

At 10am, it begins. In a street of pebbledash semis, in the rain and wind, the band start into A Guid New Year. It's an old tune, one they always play on this day, and it incorporates the refrain from Auld Lang Syne. They walk around the streets, playing this over and over, past homes and shuttered shops, past red-brick miners' rows. It is a marvellous sound.

People come to the door, in dressing gowns and onesies, to greet the musicians. Sleepy-eyed kids watch from upstairs windows, breathing mist on to the glass and then wiping themselves a peephole. Being in this band is a badge of honour. Big Mark Conlon, a council worker in his forties, has long held an ambition to play the cornet, but has been told that his limited musical talents are best expressed in the field of percussion, which is to say jingling coins in a collection bucket which he carries door to door.

It is a tradition to call in at certain houses for a drink and a bite. We stop at the home of Alan Fernie's 85 year old father, Bob. He used to be a miner at Lady Victoria, was caretaker at the band hall, and played the big drum in these New Year's Day marches, but doesn't keep well enough any more. Everyone piles in, and Alan offers drinks: "Who's fur a Girder?" This is band code for vodka and Irn-Bru. Few say no.

Alan gives a toast, and gestures towards his father. The old man has been like a kid at Christmas, waiting for the musicians to arrive. "He's been up aw night. Seriously, I've no had a wink of sleep. When we got up this morning, he said to me, 'Ah'm no really part of the band any more, am I?' I said, 'Dad, you'll always be part of the band'."

That is deep truth. Mineshaft deep. The Silver Band, for as long as it plays music, contains within in it the breath of anyone who has ever played in it, from those Victorian miners who were among its founders to the teenagers playing in it now. The village has changed a great deal in its lifetime, but this day, this music, has been a fixed point, unchanging over the years, decade, century or so since the band was founded in 1892.

"On New Year's Day, the village comes together," says Daniel Shearer, 18 year old drummer in the band. "It's the heartbeat of Newtongrange. As a young person, you feel a responsibility to come out and help keep this going."

The day wears on to lunchtime. The band arrive at the Dean Tavern, where they are to play their annual concert. The Dean is a fascinating place, one of the last "Gothenbergs" in Scotland – meaning a pub in which the profits are paid out in support of community projects, including, in this case, the band. "Goths" were once common in mining areas, and links to the temperance movement meant that they were intended to be spartan places, so as not to encourage prolonged stays and too much bevvying.

This could not be said of the Dean, which, on New Year's Day at least, has a fair claim to being the most welcoming and attractive pub in Scotland. It's a big space full of light. On the walls: a framed picture of Robert Burns in a masonic apron, next to a signed photo of Denis Law. Punters stand four deep at the bar, and in a semi-circle around the band, who sit down to play an extraordinary feelgood repertoire including Loch Lomond, I'm Gonna Be (500 Miles), You'll Never Walk Alone.

"Walk on, walk on," everyone sings, "with hope in your heart ..." It's very moving. This is the day on which we think of the year to come, and of those we have lost.

Sheila McLeod, a woman in the crowd, turns to say hello. She's from Gorebridge. Her father died a few months before, she explains. He was 93 and had worked in the pits for 44 years. He had loved the old Waverley train route, and had travelled on it as a boy with his three siblings, spending summers with grandparents in Hawick. Sheila had hoped to take him on the Borders Railway, to recreate a flavour of these boyhood trips, but it wasn't to be. He missed it by a year.

She'll take the train in his memory, though, accompanying his younger brother Dave, her uncle. Dave Ramage is 85 and here today. He remembers the names of all the stops between Gorebridge and Hawick – Fushiebridge, Tynehead, Heriot, Foutainhall, Stow, Belses, Hassendean; "wonderful wee stations," he can see them all yet. He remembers the sound of the train horn, and the strange silence following closure in 1969. He remembers, too, making a trip in 1975 to see the railway bridge out of Hawick blown up, and how resistant it seemed to being destroyed; contractors had to dynamite it twice. "It didn't want to go. I thought, 'Well done, old bridge.'"

Mr Ramage, like the Lothianbridge Viaduct, like the Nitten Silver Band, like an old song of auld acquaintance, knows what it is to endure. "My 86th birthday is in September," he says, "and I would like to think I'll make the journey from Gorebridge to the Borders again."

* * *

"WAVERLEY" was the name chosen by the North British Railway Company for the 98 and a quarter mile train line from Edinburgh to Carlisle which opened on July 1st, 1862. A century of use and almost half a century of absence has meant that nostalgic memories, some joyful, some melancholy, cling to the word like burrs. But from the start it was romantic name, and deliberately so.

The line passed within a mile of Sir Walter Scott's home, Abbotsford, and took its name from his series of novels, as a marketing ploy. He had been dead 30 years by the time the line opened, but remained a hugely popular writer, influencing the way we see Scotland. Our perception of the land viewed from the window of a train passing through the Borders as "picturesque" would not be exactly the same had Scott not existed. Many of the steam locomotives which

once sped up and down the line were given names out of Scott – Wandering Willie, The Talisman, Redgauntlet, Wizard Of The Moor.

A lovely NBR poster of 1907 offered English passengers the chance to experience, "The Home and Haunts of Sir Walter Scott", without having to sacrifice any comforts. These trains, it promised, came complete with, "Dining Cars, Sleeping Cars, and Lavatory Carriage".

Today's rail travellers can now visit Abbotsford again. The Borders Railway terminus of Tweedbank is a 20 minute walk from Scott's former home, and it is hoped to start a regular minibus service to and from the station in time for the 2016 season.

It is well worth the trip. Abbotsford is a glowering phantasmagoria, Disnae-land Castle, all turrets and towers and tartanalia; to walk just its entrance hall, sun slanting through the stained glass and on to suits of armour, and walrus skulls, and broadswords from Culloden, is to know yourself in one of Scotland's extraordinary places. Scott started to build it in 1817, and he died here on September 21st, 1832. You can visit the study, where he wrote his later novels, working with feverish honour to pay off huge debts, and you can examine with awe – but not touch – his desk, quill and spectacles. The impression is that Scott has just stepped away for a moment, soon to return.

"Scott called Abbotsford a conundrum, a flibbertigibbet of a place," says Hamish Reid, 70, a volunteer guide, "and what I think is the best description: a novel set it in stone."

Following Scott's death, Abbotsford was opened to the public, but his family continued to live in private apartments in one wing. This remained the case until the death, in 2004, of his great-great-great-granddaugher Dame Jean Maxwell Scott, who had herself inherited the property from her sister, Lady Patricia. Visitor numbers had been on the slide for a while, and there followed a period during which its future was in doubt. There were fears it would close for lack of money, but, since 2007, it has been under the care of a charitable trust, and in 2013, following restoration, it was reopened by the Queen.

There is a sense, visiting Abbotsford, that once a thing arrives in the house, it is there to stay. This is as true of the staff as it is of Rob Roy's dirk. "I came to help out for two weeks, 38 years ago," laughs Jeanette McWhinnie. That was 1977, when she was 30, and although her title is now Senior Administrator, she seems to have had every job going, starting in the tea room and working her way up.

Her family and Scott's go back a long way. Her grandfather and great-grandfather were foresters on the estate. Her mother was a friend of the Maxwell-Scotts, neither of whom had children, and she herself grew close to them. "Mrs Patricia was like a second mum to me," she recalls, "and I was actually with Dame Jean when she died. She had been in the Edinburgh Royal Infirmary; we managed to get her back home here, and she passed away then."

According to McWhinnie, the sisters had felt that Abbotsford was their home, but never their house. It belonged, they believed, to the nation. McWhinnie shares this view, and is very aware of the responsibility of carrying Scott's legacy into the future. She enjoys seeing visitors arrive, and tries not to mind too much when daft tourists think they're visiting the home of Scott of the Antarctic, or, worse, Sir Walter Raleigh. "They wondered where the cloak was," she sighs, "that he put across the puddle."

Outside, in the garden, as the Saltire flies from a turret, Jo Swiers is enjoying the sun. Abbotsford sits on the banks of the Tweed, at the centre of a 110-acre estate made up of woodland and formal gardens. Swiers, 45, is one of the gardeners. She has lived in Scotland for most of her life, but is from Yorkshire originally, a fact made plain both in her accent and her splendid flat cap.

She loves it here, and feels the presence of Scott as she goes about her daily work, talking about him, sometimes, in the present tense – "His bedroom window looks out across that side, and he can see the garden" – and detecting his personal stamp in the way the gardens have been laid out. She has noticed some Spanish Chestnuts which she believes he planted – "He probably heeled them in" – and considers this a "living link" with the writer.

Scott seems to have taken a keener interest in gardening late in life. Following his wife's death, he visited the London nursery of Lee and Kennedy, and spent a great deal of money on seeds and flowers. Swiers believes he may have found consolation, in his grief, in the garden. Certainly, it is a tranquil, beautiful spot, unmistakably his. A sculpture in the sunken garden beside the house shows the kneeling form of the traitor John Morris, a character from the novel Rob Roy, pleading for his life in a patch of honeysuckle.

"You're so aware that you are walking around in Scott's footsteps," says Swiers.

"Everywhere you go, he's walked in front of you."
     Now, it's easier for all of us to walk there, too. Take the "Waverley" line and go.

* * *

THE Melrose Sevens. One Saturday in April. Always a big day out in the Borders.
In a culture where rugby is close to being a faith, this is a sacred gathering. In
days gone by, special trains would run from all the Borders towns, as folk came
to see their team compete for one of the sport's greatest prizes; and, who knows,
perhaps those days will come again. Anyway, regardless of how people get here,
and God knows how they plan – beerily, blearily – to get home, they have come
in their thousands and are intent on the good time to end all good times.
     Seven-a-side rugby is now a global phenomenon. The world's first tournament
was played in the Borders town of Melrose in 1883. The idea was simply to boost
the club's finances, the idea being that more games could be played in one day
if the sides were reduced from the traditional fifteen men.

What began in a spirit of thrift, survives in a spirit of pride. There are now Sevens events all round the Borders in April and May, but to win at Melrose is still the grand dream. The Greenyards ground is, in its unassuming way, one of the most wonderful amphitheatres in world sport. Stand at the furthest corner of the park and you can look back beyond the main stand to the great glowering humps of the Eildons. At this time of year, the whins are coming into flower, meaning that even the hills wear the black and gold uniform of the home side.

It is a rather unsettled day. Dark clouds scud over Melrose Abbey, where Robert the Bruce's heart is said to be buried. There is a smell of cut grass, and the skirl of bagpipes. The town has gone rugby daft. Mannequins in the window display of a fashion boutique clutch balls in the crooks of their elegant arms.

At 11am, the crowds start to arrive, many of them in fancy dress, deely boppers whipping in the stiff breeze. A group of six middle-aged men dressed as Elvis Presley, and singing Viva Las Vegas, explain that they have travelled up from Wakefield. Last year they came as nuns. "It's the most prestigious and historic rugby tournament in the world," explains one, "so, naturally, we decided to dignify the occasion by dressing up as the king of rock 'n' roll."

evens 9th April 20
w.melrose7s.com

Some of the punters seem, already, unsteady on their feet, and increasingly so as the day wears on. It is forbidden to bring a carry-out into the ground, but some have found a way around it. Some boisterous twentysomething Melrosians, to get around paying bar prices, have rigged up a complicated apparatus involving rubber tubing attached to what look an awful lot like colostomy bags hidden inside their clothes. These contain neat vodka, and the group of pals huddle round, taking turns to sook on the nozzle. The demure young women of town, after a few snorts of this illicit hooch, are ready to exchange confidences in the toilet queue. "Here," says one, "ah've been pishin' like a horse aw day."

In the clubhouse, with its silverware, and its sepia photographs of great teams past, two Melrose worthies are holding court in blazers and club ties. Jack Dun is 88; George Bunyan, ten years younger, is just a boy. These men, between them, have missed the Sevens on just six occasions since 1934. Dun reckons he is the only person left alive to have seen Jock Allan play rugby. A Melrose man, he kicked five goals against England at Murrayfield on March 21st, 1931; the ball with which

he did it is on display in this very room, a holy relic, only slightly deflated. "Aye," says Bunyan, "rugby is virtually a religion here."

The Greenyards is a promised land of tartan rugs and shooting sticks. Rugby WAGs in skinny jeans, quilted Barbours and Ray-Bans throw their tweed blankets aside and leap up, shrieking, "Come on!", as their particular beau nears the tryline. There are 24 teams in competition here today. Some, notably squads from Tobago and the USA, bring a touch of glamour with their dreadlocks and stars 'n' stripes skullcaps. But, inevitably, Borders supremacy asserts itself; a triumph of genetics and inherited characteristics – all that neckless, fearless, thunder-thighed, lightning-brained, ruddy-cheeked, bloody-minded DNA spiralling through several generations of braw and brawny lads. The international visitors are soon put out.

Up in the press box, a shoogly rookery on top of the main stand, the air smells of coffee and whisky. Journalists work in intense bursts, rushing to file match reports while the internet connection lasts. Every time the wi-fi goes down, so, too, does the level on a bottle of Grouse. This is also the domain of Dr Iain Houston, a small man in his mid-70s, in a blazer and tartan trews, binoculars slung round his neck. His job is to make announcements over the public address system, which he does between mouthfuls of mutton pie. Mr Houston has an admirably dry manner about him. "If the owner of the black Hyundai which was parked outside the Abbey will go to the police station," he says, "you will learn something to your advantage."

Come teatime, it's all over. The final is won by Glasgow, Melrose having been put out in the semis. The locals will have to wait a little longer for a home triumph, but everyone's had a great day for all that, not least the lads from Wakefield, who head away back down the road after a grand day out, quiffs limp but spirits high, following one last rendition of Viva Las Vegas. The Sevens are finished for another

year. The Greenyards lies empty. Elvis, Elvis, Elvis, Elvis, Elvis and Elvis have left the building.

* * *

"TRADITION is all we've got left in the Borders," says Jim Amos, a 66 year with a neat white beard who has been town crier in Galashiels for 29 years. "Our mills are away, our industry's away, but we've got this."

This is the Braw Lads' Gathering – the annual ceremony which has taken place in Galashiels, usually in the last week of June, since 1930. It is the proudest day

in the town's calendar, and is part of a cycle of Common Ridings, similar equestrian festivals which take place throughout the summer in the Borders towns. Each town, naturally, considers their ceremony to be the best, and each is a little different from the others. Hawick, a large town to the south which has long been the great rival of Galashiels, is the first Common Riding of the season; awash in the traditional beverage rum 'n' milk, it has the quality of a bacchanal. The Braw Lads' Gathering is, by contrast, a rather more solemn occasion – no less deeply felt, but a little quieter, more delicate, not quite so wild. Wonderful, though. "This," says Andrew Johnston, President of the Gathering, "is our moment of magic."

The magic begins at 8am, at the town's handsome Burgh Chambers. It rained a little the night before – "Just enough to keep the stoor doon," observes one seasoned weather-watcher – but the morning is already warm.

Inside the Victorian building, this year's Braw Lad – 23 year old Gavin Young – is sitting on a wooden bench, holding his speech in white-gloved hands, mouthing the words, nerves radiating off him in waves. This is his big day, the town's big day, and he doesn't want to risk any mistakes. The bench has these words carved into it, "There's Nae Place Like Hame", a phrase that speaks top the Wizard Of Oz transformation these Borders towns undergo on Common Riding day – their auld grey stone transformed by a riot of colour and pageantry. Young is an agricultural sales rep in everyday life, but there's nothing everyday about Galashiels on this day. In his check breeks and black bonnet, carrying the flag and wearing a sash, a whip strapped across his back, the Braw Lad is a local hero – representative of the town's proud past and hopeful future.

"It's the biggest honour you can receive," he explains. "I've always wanted to be the Braw Lad, from a very young age, from the minute I got on a horse." He shakes his head, as if in pity of any poor soul unfortunate to come from outwith Galashiels. "If you're not from the Borders, you'll never understand."

The Braw Lads' Gathering commemorates a number of events from the town's history, from skirmishes with the English in the 14th century to the sacrifice of the Second World War. It's true meaning, though, is as a celebration of community.

There are six principals in the ceremony, who spend the day travelling on horseback around the town and its environs – the Braw Lad, the Brass Lass (19 year old beauty therapist, Alice Mackay) and their four attendants. In a historic first, Alice's big sister Nicola, herself a previous Braw Lass, is also a principal – the Bearer of the White Roses. Richard Mackay, father of Alice and Nicola, is the

local tailor who makes the outfits for the principals. It was his duty and distinct pleasure this year to make the white uniform for his younger daughter. "The whites are effectively a wedding dress. She wears them once and she won't wear them again," he says. "I don't cry often, but there's a tear in my eye today."

By tradition, the other Borders towns send envoys to each Common Riding, so Gala – as it is known – is hoaching with young men in a variety of striking outfits: bowlers and toppers, sashes and spurs. These other principals are the

equivalents, in their own towns, of the Braw Lad and Lass here: the Whipman from West Linton; the Hawick Cornet; the Bari Manushi and Bari Gadgi from Yetholm. There are so many rosettes of so many different colours that one might mistake this for a by-election in a key marginal. Kelso rosettes are the biggest, like dinner plates, but those from Melrose have by the far the longest ribbons, at around three feet. Don't ask why. "It's aye been," is what you'll be told, the standard stonewall response to any daft outsider's enquiry. This phrase, never far from a Borderers lips, articulates the devotion to tradition that characterises this part of Scotland. Things have always been like this, so why change? These towns are bonded to their own past like an infant coorying into its mother.

The Braw Lads' Gathering is a rollercoaster with several peaks. There are spectacular moments, such as when several hundred riders on horseback ford the Tweed, or, later, when those same riders gallop up the steep hill of Scott Street, the clattering of their hooves all but drowned out by cheers. The crowds packed on to pavements on both sides of the street have a literary quality. The women are straight out of Jilly Cooper, all posh frocks and fascinators. The men are Wodehousian in tweeds and ruddy cheeks.

An emotional high-point is reached with the ceremony known as the Mixing of the Roses, which takes place on a raised platform at the Old Town Cross. Commemorating the 1503 marriage of James IV to Margaret Tudor, it is a moment of slow and solemn choreography, observed in silence by hundreds of townsfolk huddled together in the streets. Nicola Mackay, on bended knee, hands red and then white roses up to her sister, Alice, who arranges them together and places them at the cross. Afterwards, both are in tears, overcome by the occasion. The town crier bellows, "God save the Queen!", and a Shih Tzu, its top-knot tied up in black and white ribbon – Gala colours – yaps approval of the sentiment.

"I can't describe it," Alice says, later. "The bonds that I have with sister are so strong, and that feeling of her giving me my roses ... I'm welling up thinking about it. There's no better feeling."

* * *

THERE is a saying in the Borders about the Common Ridings: "It's better felt than telt". This is quite true. It can be difficult for those of us who come from outside the area to truly understand what these ceremonies mean, or indeed the feeling that those who live there have for their land and their towns. The people of Newtongrange might understand it, though; or the Gorebridge folk; and Melrosians certainly will. At heart, it is about reclaiming the word parochialism – understanding that it is no bad thing to know a place intimately and for that knowledge, with the passing years, to deepen and become love.

This Borders mindset is informed, in part, by a sense of isolation. This is more felt than real, although the closure of the Waverley Line in 1969 did leave Hawick and Galashiels further from the rail network than any other towns of their size in mainland Britain, exacerbating that sensation of being at a remove from the rest of the world.

There is an ancient foundation to that feeling: the region having been squeezed up out of the sea bed millions of years ago as the land-masses which would become Scotland and England drifted towards each other. The Borders, therefore, belongs to neither. "Hawick was ever independent," run the words of a favourite song, and the song, geologically speaking, is true.

This independence of spirit, this feeling that the Borders stand alone, runs too deep to be changed by the coming of the trains. The Borders Railway, rather, offers an opportunity to the rest of us to better appreciate what the locals know – that this is one of the world's special places. Robert the Bruce left his heart here, and now we can, too.

T HEY called him King Richard. The chairman of the North British Railway, Richard Hodgson, was a businessman with the dread air of a Shakespearean monarch. The Times newspaper marvelled at his "imperial will". The Spectator, in November, 1866, noted that he was, "Resolute, remorseless and one-idead, a man utterly unscrupulous when needful". By that year, by that man, the Waverley Route had recently been completed – a colossal, ambitious project, linking Edinburgh with Carlisle, through some of the bleakest, most difficult, hostile countryside in the British Isles.

The new Borders Railway is an echo of this line, a clang resonating into the 21st century. The Waverley Route was built in two stages. The first, Edinburgh to Hawick, was completed in 1849, based in part on the much earlier Edinburgh & Dalkeith line, which had been known as "The Innocent Railway", supposedly because no fatal accidents had ever taken place on it. Work began on the second stage, Hawick to Carlisle, in the autumn of 1859 and was completed on July 1st, 1862. From 1876 trains were able to run through from Edinburgh Waverley to London St Pancras.

"We have no hesitation in saying that no railway in the United Kingdom lies through such scenery ..." declared one London newspaper at the time. "We doubt whether there is any other of which it can be said that it would be worth while to travel on it for the sake of the scenery alone, but we have no hesitation to assert this of the Waverley Route."

So, it was bonnie. But it was born out of sweat and tears, and the rank smell of risked fortunes. This was a period of intense competition between the private railway companies of the time. The North British, led by Hodgson, wanted to get to Carlisle. The Caledonian, which already operated between Glasgow and Carlisle, was determined to stop that happening. There followed a period of lobbying Parliament and attempting to stoke up local support. In the summer of 1858, Richard Hodgson spoke at a public dinner in Hawick, telling 600 guests of his determination to build the railway south from Hawick. It was a speech worthy of the Battle of Britain, of Agincourt. "I will truckle to no one," he said. "I will go forward as long as I have strength, and have no fear that we will be successful in the end."

He had his way. The railway was given royal assent on July 21st, 1859. The people of Hawick, hearing this news, are said to have poured out of their homes and mills into the streets. Flags were hung from windows, and bonfires lit as the celebrations continued into the night. When the ceremonial cutting of the first sod took place in the late summer of that year, Hawick enjoyed a public holiday. A

mahogany wheelbarrow and silver spade was carried aloft on the shoulders of four navvies in white jackets. It is unlikely that they wore these jackets during the work itself, or, if they did, that they remained white for long.

Building the Waverley Route was brutal, not helped by the wet and miserable winters of 1859 and 1860, or by the high and twisting landscape through which the line had to pass. Building materials were dragged across the moors by horses. Navvies at Whitrope were soaked by the estimated 400 gallons of water which poured into the tunnel each minute, and two of these men are buried there. Other deaths occurred at Bowshank, Stow and Burnfoot. In 1846, near Gorebridge, a mob of navvies murdered a policeman, Richard Pace.

Out of this bloody crucible, an extraordinary railway came. It was a testing ground for the men who worked on it. "With two summits of around 900-1000 feet, and a serpentine succession of curves throughout, the 98 miles of the Waverley Route was arguably the most operationally difficult line in Britain," wrote AJ Mullay in his book, Rails Across The Border. It was, observed the railway writer OS Nock, "no place for weak or ailing engines".

Harry Knox from Linlithgow knows all about that. He began his career in the railway in 1956 at the age of sixteen, retiring from the industry in 2006, having occupied a senior position within British Rail in Glasgow. However, as a young man, he had the pleasure and privilege of shovelling coal into engines on the Waverley Route in the last days of steam.

The Falahill summit is the highest point of the Borders Railway at 880 feet above sea level. Knox remembers well the effort it took to get a train at coaches up a 1 in 70 gradient that lasted for nearly miles. His shirt, he says, was nothing but a wet rag stuck to his back. "It really was non-stop shovelling," he says. One might shovel a quarter of a ton of coal getting to the top of the hill.

"The sweat was literally running off me," Knox recalls. "A stream off my nose. That really was the hallmark of firing steam engines. You were working in front of a fire that was between two and three thousand degrees. So, yes, we expended a lot of fluid on the footplate."

Hard graft, then, but well-earned joy, too. "When you got over the top at Falahill it was like a Sunday," says Knox. "You sat down and enjoyed going down alongside the Gala Water. There was very little steam being used. So, after you'd got your fire repaired, you could sit and have a cup of tea and enjoy the scenery." There is something winningly presbyterian about this: the promise of paradise following a period of labour and pain.

Knox was based, in those days, at the locomotive depot in Haymarket, where the passenger trains which ran on the Waverley Route were based. The depot had opened in 1894 and by the late 1950s remained essentially Victorian in appearance and atmosphere. "Dickensian" is the word Knox uses. Dante's Inferno, he feels, is a reasonable comparison — all smoke and flame-lit darkness. It was a place that was never at rest, and the noise was incredible. The hiss of steam. The clang of metal on metal. No one just spoke. You had to shout to be heard. And the smell? That was something else. Quite a concoction. The usual railway aroma — hot oil and the rest, but also a stink peculiar to that part of Edinburgh: the chemical plant where they manufactured ether; the brewery and distillery; the North British Rubber Company; burnt sugar from the sweetie factory; and, of course, the glue works, where hides and bones and hooves became a sticky witches' brew. "Haymarket," laughs Knox, "certainly added to the reek of Auld Reekie."

That nearly half a century has passed since the Waverley Route was closed means that such vivid first-hand accounts of what it was like to work on the line are growing ever more scarce. So one must thank the gods of fire and steam and steel for preserving Louie Gracie, who is 83, and remains in love with the engines he fell for as a child and to which he devoted his working life. Mr Gracie is a dapper man in shirt and tie and braces; railway signals embroidered on his socks. A painting above the fireplace in his Bonnyrigg home shows a black V2 locomotive, one on which he worked, stopped at Whitrope siding. "Those," he says, with some pride, "were the finest things that ever ran on rails."

Gracie started out as an engine cleaner, was a fireman between 1949 and 1970, worked as a driver when the diesels came in, and ended up as a chief traction inspector, retiring in the late 1990s. He loved the days of steam best. When he stands up to demonstrate the correct way to shovel coal into a firebox, it becomes clear that muscle memory and visual memory are working as one; he remembers every bit of the Waverley Route — how it looked, how it felt, how the wheels squealed on tight bends — and no doubt could, if pressed, take a locomotive down it now. "Listen to a steam engine when you're driving," he says. "She speaks to you. She tells you what she wants and what she disnae want."

It wasn't just a job to him. It was a calling. He remembers all sorts. He remembers, one very hot day, perhaps in the 1950s, coming into a wee station south of Gala and alarming a party of nuns gathered on the station because he was stripped to the waist and leaning out the cab. He remembers, too, taking the doctor from Hawick to Riccarton, a village accessible only by rail, to attend patients.

Riccarton has been abandoned for many years. There is almost nothing there now, save the ruin of the station master's house. I show Gracie a photo of this on my phone, and his customary cheer abandons him at the sight.

"Oh, in the name of goodness," he says. "Jesus. Can hardly believe that, eh?"

* * *

RICCARTON Junction should be on the itinerary of those interested in the history of the Waverley Route, and anyone with a taste for the elegiac. Roughly equidistant south of Hawick and north of Newcastleton, Riccarton was once a busy place, if isolated, and is now a lost village, a sort of post-industrial St Kilda.

You get there by walking south for about half an hour, down the line of the lifted track, from the Whitrope Heritage Centre, just off the B6399, in an area of the Scottish Borders for which the expression "middle of nowhere" is scarcely adequate. You will be accompanied on your walk by the shush of a burn, but more often by unsettling silence. Buzzards wheel overhead, idling in gyres. Broken, mossy footbridge stanchions bring Ozymandias to mind. A milepost, paint peeling, pokes out from the side of a cutting, to inform passers-by that Edinburgh is 66 miles to the north. Not far by train, perhaps, but it has been a long time since the last.

Riccarton itself is a lonely, even eerie spot. A mind that runs naturally to ghosts will find much to occupy itself, especially when surveying the roofless shell of the station master's house. Was anyone born here? Did anyone die here? The village had over 150 residents in its heyday. A school, a post office, a Co-op, a smart red telephone box. This place was built for railway workers, and until 1963 – when that forestry track was cleared – there was no access at all, except by train. The railway was, therefore, both the purpose and the lifeline of Riccarton – and, eventually, its downfall. When, in 1969, the Waverley Route closed, the community was abandoned. A cheery blue and white platform sign, put there by the Whitrope Heritage volunteers, is almost all that is left to indicate that Riccarton ever existed; Skara Brae, the stone-age village in Orkney, appears to have been more recently inhabited. Louie Gracie remembered that when engines stopped here, the firemen would sometimes dash off and into the shop on an errand to buy fags for the driver. It's hard to imagine that now. Riccarton is long gone. All smoke extinguished.

David Spaven, the railway historian, used to visit Riccarton as a child, on camping holidays, by train from Edinburgh, with his father and brother. This was in the 1960s. "For a young trainspotter and railway enthusiast who liked the natural environment, it was just a wonderful place to be," he recalls. "For a city-dweller it was absolutely fascinating, almost literally another world." When the line closed, he vowed never to return to Riccarton, and so, in his memory, it is preserved just as it was.

Spaven is the author of Waverley Route – The Life, Death and Rebirth of the Borders Railway, an authoritative and detailed account of the closure and campaign for reopening. The line was, in his view, "the most undeserved victim of the infamous Beeching Axe". The Beeching Report of 1963 called for savings to be made in public spending by the closure of 2,000 stations across Britain and passenger services to be withdrawn from 5,000 miles of line. When the Waverley Route closed, on January 6th, 1969, the Borders region was home to the largest population in Britain to live at such a distance from the railway. Around 70,000 people were now more than 25 miles from their nearest station. This has brought about and intensified, many argue, depopulation and economic decline in the area. The grim joke was if you didn't die waiting for the bus from Hawick to Edinburgh, you would surely pass away during the journey. It was, as locals said, quicker by hearse.

The railway was not taken away without a fight. One doughty campaigner was Madge Elliot, now in her eighties, but then a wife and mother with a young family, determined to play her part in keeping the trains running. Madge is a proud Terie, as folk from Hawick are pleased to call themselves, but more than that she is a "guiter-bluid", meaning she was born in the oldest part of town, and – according to legend – the bloody afterbirth tossed in the gutter. In other words, Hawick through and through.

Gathering almost 12,000 signatures on a petition to save the railway, Elliot and a few other campaigners took the train to London a few days before Christmas in 1968, played into Downing Street by a piper giving laldy to Blue Bonnets Over The Border. The petition was wrapped up in red paper, for the ruling Labour Party, and bound with funereal black ribbon. Inside Number Ten, Elliot felt her knees knocking together with nerves, but she calmed down by reminding herself that the Prime Minister was only there at the will of the people. She handed over the petition to a flunky, who said he would make sure Harold Wilson saw it, and that was that. She had done all she could. It had been a struggle, and she hadn't felt supported by the local men of influence; one senior councillor, she recalls, had phoned to say, "Mrs Elliot, you're wasting your time. You should just go back to your housewife's duties."

Madge Elliot was not successful in keeping the line open. But she does not feel it was a waste of time to try. One ought to stand up the things one feels are important. She is pleased that the line is reopening, at least as far as Tweedbank, though her feelings seem a little bittersweet. "What a damned waste," she says. "It should never have closed in the first place. If the Hawick folk want it to come here in future, they'll have to fight for it. But I winna be leading the fight. Not at my age. It's up to them. I tried my best. We didna succeed, but they kent we were there."

The campaign to keep the line open also saw an extraordinary incident on the evening of Sunday January 5th, 1969. The last passenger service down the Waverley Route to London left Edinburgh at 2156. Little did the driver Willie Fleming and fireman George Paterson know that they were heading into a storm. The journey to Hawick passed without incident, the train arriving at just before half past eleven at night. A crowd of around 200, including Madge Elliot, had gathered on the southbound platform to load a cardboard coffin on to the guard's van. It was addressed to the Minister of Transport and was marked with this solemn epitaph: "Waverley Line – Born 1849, Killed 1969 – aged 120 years."

Just after midnight, the train went on its way. Arriving in Newcastleton, just short of the border with England, the sleeper was held up by protestors. Led by the Reverend Brydon Maben, the local minister, a crowd of people, a few hundred strong, forced the gates of a level crossing closed, preventing the train making further progress, despite the best efforts of the police.

David Steel, then a young MP, was on board, making his way to Westminster. "I had actually gone to bed on the train," he recalls. "One of the station staff came along, shouting for me. I opened the window and he said, 'Could you come and speak to the crowd?' I had to get dressed again. It was a bitterly cold night. The police had arrested the parish minister, and that only made the situation worse. It was getting on for two in the morning, so I said to the crowd that if I could get the minister released without any charges, would they agree to go away, having made their point? So that was agreed, and I went round to the police station, and we got him out. The train arrived about three hours late at St Pancras."

It would be fascinating to know what the experience was like for the driver and fireman involved. Both men have since died, and no personal accounts of that night have come to light. Even their first names were unrecorded until now. Willie Fleming, the driver, was the elder. You can see him leaning out of the cab in a famous photograph taken when the train was held up at Newcastleton. Colleagues who remember Fleming from the depot in Edinburgh recall him as "a cheery lad, always laughing and joking, nothing serious about him" and "a very competent driver".

Punctuality was in the blood of railwaymen, coiling through their very DNA, but those who knew Fleming think it unlikely that he would have been upset at being made late by the protestors. Rather, he may well have had sympathy for their cause. Louie Gracie "fired to" Willie Fleming, meaning that he shovelled coal into the firebox on some of his trains, and recalls that many workers of the time lost their jobs. ""It was a sad day for them when that railway shut," he says. "They did not want it to go."

George Paterson, the fireman on that last service, was born in 1925, lived in Clermiston with his wife and two sons, and died at the age of 66, a year after leaving the railway. "Och, he was dedicated to the cause. He just loved his work," says his son, Derek. "He was on the railway most of his life, and found difficulty in retirement because of that. He was at a bit of a loss."

Photo: Courtesy of Bruce McCartney.

4 June 2015: Madge Elliot MBE unveils the nameplate on the Freightliner locomotive bearing her name. The ceremony was planned to mark the completion of the Borders Railway construction works. (Photo: Alan Harvey, SNS)

Paterson was, by all accounts, a quiet man, a family man. A man with a sense of duty. Derek remembers him going to his work in dungarees and a peaked cap. Later, when he became a driver, he wore a three-piece uniform. He was a mentor to young men coming into the industry, and was always happy to encourage the firemen and drivers of the future. The year after the Waverley Route closed, he spent time across the Atlantic, working as a fireman on that famous steam locomotive, The Flying Scotsman, which was much the same age as him, on its American and Canadian tour. Personal photographs of the time show him happy amongst the valves and pipes and flames. "He was obsessed with the railway. He lived and breathed it," says his son, Derek.

The Waverley Route, however, lived and breathed no more.

* * *

THE years passed. The decades. In place of a line grew a legend. That word, "Waverley" had always been intended to give the route an air of historical romance, but this feeling intensified with closure. The line died before its time, like a tragic poet or pop star, and this gave it a certain doomed, nostalgic appeal.

In 1999, the Campaign for Borders Rail was established to make the case for restoring the railway to the area. The cause gathered support and momentum, but progress was slow. For a long time it looked as though the only bit of the line that would ever be rebuilt would be that being constructed, painstakingly slowly, by the Waverley Route Heritage Association – a group of ardent, hardy volunteers – who have laid, by hand, a short section of track, from near the southern end of the Whitrope tunnel, on which they run trains, May to October, for the enjoyment of the public and themselves. "It's that obdurate British spirit," says Duncan Thomas, vice-chairman of the association. "You can take a lot of pride in saying, 'No, you're not getting rid of this. We're going to rebuild this thing.'"

It was in the summer of 2006, that the Scottish Parliament passed a bill to reconstruct the railway to Tweedbank. In 2011, Network Rail was named by the government as the firm to deliver the project. Main construction work began in the spring of 2013.

No one could truthfully claim that the rebuilding project has gone entirely smoothly or that everyone has been happy about it. There are those who consider the whole thing a waste of money and are sceptical about the line's ability to drive tourism or boost the Borders economy. Others, who welcome the railway, are disappointed that more of it is not double-tracked, and that it terminates at Tweedbank rather than continuing to Hawick, Melrose, or even on to Carlisle.

There are those, too, who live along the route of the new line, so have had to put up with the construction work, but do not have a station at the end of it. These are the people who have experienced a dark variation on WH Auden's famous poem: this is the railway down to the Borders, bringing unchecked noise and disorder.

In the tiny settlement of Falahill, a run of ten houses now marooned between the railway and the A7, they complain of repeated disruptions to the water supply and homes shaking or even damaged by blasting work. In Fountainhall, the problems have been to do with dirt on the roads and in the air, and worries over a lack of privacy as workmen and — soon — trains pass along the tracks at eye-level with bedroom windows; one woman says she has had to keep her blinds down for a year. In Heriot, they have been angered by traffic disruption and by a new underpass which, residents say, has flooded again and again. The talk, in all these places, is of invasion and imposition; a sense that the railway is something which has happened to them, against their will.

"It's a war zone," says one member of Heriot Community Council. "We're just collateral damage, and we really haven't mattered in the process."

On September 6, when the Borders Railway opens, the past will be over and the future will begin. That Sunday, the first train will carry a freight of memories — good and bad. All those old ghosts. King Richard Hodgson will be on board. Willie Fleming and George Paterson. Reverend Brydon Maben. The lost folk of Riccarton. It will be exciting and emotions will run high. For all that there are some who loathe the railway, others regard its return as having a sort of moral force. "There are three things I wanted to see in my lifetime," said one man in Galashiels, during the Braw Lad ceremony, "Scottish independence, the end of apartheid in South Africa, and the return of trains to the Borders."

The tale of the railway has been one of hope and stubborn will, as well as anger and perceived injustice. It has been so much more than a dull account of civil engineering and capital infrastructure. People have given their lives to this thing, and it feels proper, therefore, as an act of barter, to offer the last word to Madge Elliot, who has spent so much of her own long life longing for the day when the hills and valleys of the Borders would, once again, echo with the sound of passing trains. She knows, better than anyone, perhaps, that this is a story of resurrection.

"The railway's deid," says Madge, "but it winna lie doon."

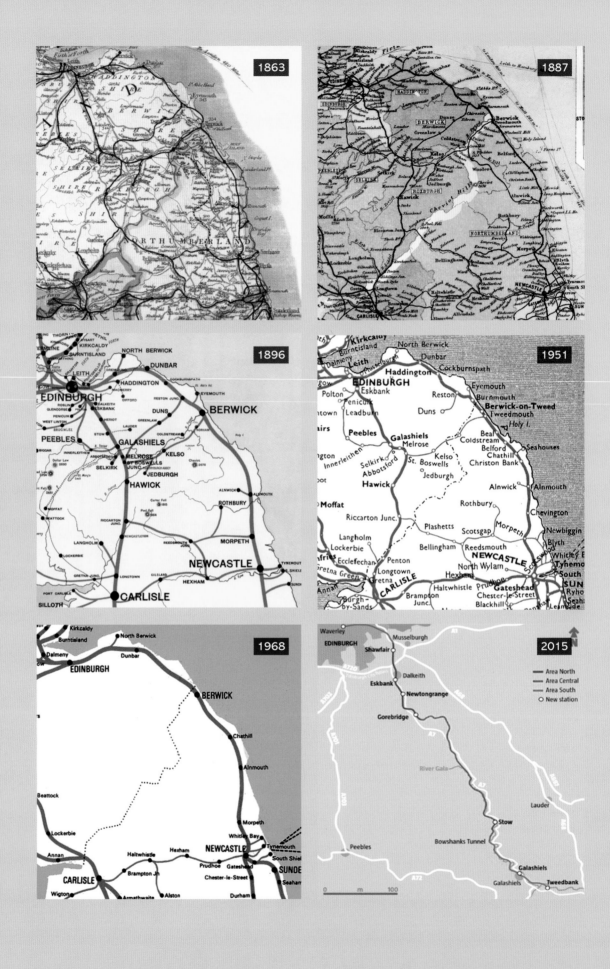

Borders Railway Fast Facts

Track

Total line length = 49km
Dynamic passing loops (x3) = 16km
Rail track laid = 65km (includes passing loops)
Slab track = 560m in Bowshank Tunnel
Switches & crossings = 7 units
Sleepers used = 95,834
Sleepers spread = 1km per day
Rails laid each day = 1.2km (or 24 X 108m rails)
Rails used = over 1,000
Rail installation team = 14 members
Top ballast spread by train = 1,800 tons per shift from 30 autohoppers
Tamping = 2km per shift
Automated Finishing Machine = 3.5km per shift
Stressing & welding = 700m per shift
Stressed temperature = 80 degrees Fahrenheit

Infrastructure

1,500,000 tonnes of earthworks
95 bridges refurbished
42 new bridges constructed
2 Victorian tunnels repaired
50km of new fencing
10km of new roads
7 Switches & Crossing units
1,100 workers at peak construction
400km of holes drilled for mining remediation
Over 3 million man hours
Longest new bridge to be built from scratch was Hardengreen Viaduct at 71.5 metres
Estimated 50,000 bacon rolls consumed by the team

Digital

Over 100,000 video plays
320,000 users visited the website
2.2m web page views
3,700 twitter followers
Over 4,500 people subscribed to e-bulletin

Correspondence

4,500 copies of 'Connections' newsletter delivered quarterly
Over 100,000 letters have been issued to residents along the line of route

Community

2,500 people attended community events
72 projects have benefited from the community fund
1,500 primary school pupils attended safety workshops delivered by Scottish Youth Theatre
7,600 boys and girls across Midlothian and Scottish Borders attended Scottish Football Association activities
150 community events attended by the project team

BIBLIOGRAPHY

Peacock, Bill, Waverley Route Reflections (Cheviot Publications, 1983)

Holland, Julian, Discovering Scotland's Lost Railways (Waverley Books, 2009)

Knox, Harry, Steam Days At Haymarket – The Collected Reminiscences of Shed Life both on and off the Footplate (Irwell Press, 2007)

Mullay, A.J., Rails Across The Border: The Story Of Anglo-Scottish Railways (Patrick Stephens Ltd, 1990)

Nock, O.S., Railway Race To The North (Ian Allan, 1958)

Perkins, Roy G. and MacIntosh, Iain, The Waverley Route Through Time (Amberley Publishing, 2012)

Spaven, David, Waverley Route - The Life, Death and Rebirth of the Borders Railway (Argyll Publishing, 2012)

Steel, David, Against Goliath – David Steel's Story (Weidenfeld & Nicolson, 1989)

Siviter, Patrick, Waverley – Portrait Of A Famous Route (Runpast Publishing, 1996)

Thomas, John, Forgotten Railways: Scotland (David & Charles, 1976)

Thomas, John, The North British Railway, Volume 1 (David & Charles, 1969)

Thomas, John, The North British Railway, Volume 2 (David & Charles, 1975)